Developing
es and the
l Financial
System

COMMONWEALTH SECRETARIAT

Developing Countries and the Global Financial System

Report of the Conference on Developing Countries and the Global Financial System

Lancaster House, London
22–23 June 2000

Edited by
Stephany Griffith-Jones and Amar Bhattacharya

Commonwealth Secretariat
Marlborough House
Pall Mall
London SW1Y 5HX
United Kingdom
Tel: +44 (0)20 7747 6342
Fax: +44 (0)20 7839 9081

Published by the Commonwealth Secretariat
Designed by Wayzgoose
Printed in the United Kingdom

Wherever possible, the Commonwealth Secretariat uses paper that is made
from sustainable forests or from sources that minimise the destructive impact
on the environment.

ISBN 0-85092-675-0   Price: £12.99

Contents

Foreword

We are delighted that the Commonwealth Secretariat, the World Bank and the International Monetary Fund were able to collaborate in this important conference on *Developing Countries and the International Financial System*, which was held in Lancaster House, London from June 22–23, 2000. We are most grateful to all the speakers and participants who came and shared their considerable expertise with each other and with us. In organising this conference, we made a special effort to invite very senior policy-makers from developing countries, as we hoped that the conference would offer them a valuable opportunity to define and express their views on the international financial architecture. We had two days of fruitful and thought-provoking discussion.

The subject of a new design of the international financial system has been put very high on the international agenda because of the frequency, severity and high development costs of recent financial crises. The President of the World Bank, James Wolfensohn, in his address to the Board of Governors during the IMF/World Bank Annual Meetings in Prague, 'Building an Equitable World', spoke about the global need to establish a stronger global financial architecture to deal with international financial crises and the phenomenon of instability in one country affecting us all. Horst Köhler, the IMF's Managing Director, in his address cautioned against complacency and emphasised that it was in the interest of all that the entire membership of the IMF is fully involved and takes full ownership of measures to strengthen the global financial architecture.

So far, there has been progress in a number of areas, thanks to the efforts of the international community and of the international organisations and developing countries. The conference provided an important opportunity – given the seniority and expertise of participants – to assess progress, and discuss future steps.

Even though progress on the international financial architecture has been important, it has been somewhat asymmetrical. In particular, there are three aspects where a broader approach would be beneficial. The first is the issue of capital flows. Crises such those in East Asia were caused not just by problems in the East Asian countries themselves, but to a large extent by imperfections in international capital markets which led to rapid surges and reversals of massive private flows. To deal with the problems of very large and potentially reversible capital flows, there is a clear need for better international regulation of those private capital flows. It is also arguable that there is a need for sufficiently large international provision of official liquidity to control crises within countries, and to prevent them spreading to other countries.

A second source of asymmetry in the process of international financial reform has been the limited participation of developing countries, including the main emerging market countries, in the process, especially in the decision-making fora. Clearly, the participation of developing countries in the G-22 and now the G-20 are useful steps, though these fora are mainly of a consultative nature. However, it would be a major step forward if developing countries, and development concerns, were represented in decision-making fora such as the Financial Stability Forum (FSF), to increase their relevance and legitimacy.

A third and final source of asymmetry has been the undue focus on crisis prevention and management, mainly for middle-income countries. Important as this is, it may have led us to a neglect of the equally, if not more important, issues of appropriate external financing for low-income countries. These require development finance in the form of multilateral lending, official aid and debt relief. They also need official and other assistance to attract more private capital flows. It is thus essential to broaden the debate on international financial architecture to ensure that the interests of smaller and poorer developing countries are taken into account.

Finally, we would like to draw attention to a serious source of concern for developing countries and for all those concerned with development, namely the views recently emerging, mainly from the industrialised countries, for a significant scaling down of lending by the IMF and the World Bank. As several of the papers prepared for this Conference point out, these proposals are exactly the opposite of what developing countries, and indeed the world economy, need. Amongst the crucial roles of the Bretton Woods Institutions are the provision of liquidity and of longer-term development finance. In both cases, the International Financial Institutions (IFIs) fill gaps not covered, or not yet covered, by private flows, either because private lenders or investors have temporarily withdrawn or because they are not willing to finance certain countries, sectors or projects. In addition, IFIs should surely facilitate and catalyse access to new and sustainable private flows.

Not only is it important to reaffirm the value of IFIs in today's and tomorrow's world, it is also crucial to make suggestions on how to maximise IFIs' contribution to development. Again, the Lancaster House

Conference made a significant contribution to this important discussion.

The Report of the Conference was presented at the Commonwealth Finance Ministers' Meeting in September 2000 and distributed to the IMF/World Bank Annual Meetings in Prague. We commend this volume of papers prepared for the Conference as a timely and important contribution to the debate about reform of the international financial system.

Kemal Dervis
Vice-President
Poverty Reduction and Economic
Management Network
World Bank

Dame Veronica Sutherland
Deputy Secretary-General
(Economic and Social Affairs)
Commonwealth Secretariat

Introduction

Stephany Griffith-Jones and Amar Bhattacharya

Background

As a result of the frequency, severity and high development costs of recent financial crises, the attempt to design a new international financial system, more appropriate for the needs of the twenty-first century, is high on the international agenda.

The Commonwealth Secretariat has been very active in this international discussion. Commonwealth Finance Ministers discussed issues relating to international financial reform at their 1998, 1999 and 2000 Meetings. In 1999, Commonwealth Finance Ministers mandated the Commonwealth Secretariat to monitor the international financial architecture.

To carry out this task, the Commonwealth Secretariat, jointly with the International Monetary Fund (IMF) and the World Bank, organised a high-level Conference on Developing Countries and the Global Financial System, held at Lancaster House, London, 22–23 June 2000.

A special emphasis of this meeting was to highlight the views of developing countries (and especially of their policy-makers) so as to help strengthen their voice in the discussion of a new international financial architecture. This was felt to be important because developing countries' participation in both the discussion and decision-making process of reform has so far been insufficient. A second major concern was to identify and highlight areas where progress on reform has, till now, been too limited.

More broadly, the Conference had the following four objectives, which were felt to have been successfully met:

◆   To take stock of progress in reforming the international financial architecture, especially from the perspective of developing countries;

◆   To identify concerns, both on issues currently being taken forward and on implementation, from the perspective of developing countries;

◆   To identify missing elements and gaps;

◆   To examine the future role of international financial institutions.

The Report of the Conference was an important input into the 2000 Commonwealth Finance Ministers' Meeting, which in turn contributed to the Commonwealth position at the annual IMF/World Bank meetings.

Given the high quality of both the discussions and of the background papers prepared for the Conference, it seemed that it would be useful to make them more widely available.

This introduction provides an outline of the main areas discussed and the key questions addressed in each session. The Conference Programme is given in Appendix A.

A number of the issues which were discussed in depth at the Conference, together with several of its recommendations, were taken up at the Commonwealth Finance Ministers' Meeting held in Malta in September 2000 and at meetings of the G-24 and G-20.

At their meeting in Malta, Commonwealth Finance Ministers reaffirmed the central role of the International Financial Institutions (IFIs) in supporting growth, financial stability and poverty reduction. They recognised that without IFI support private capital flows can be volatile, concentrated and inadequate for the needs of developing countries.

Commonwealth Finance Ministers also stressed the need for a more inclusive process of shaping the international financial architecture, where developing countries must be allowed a stronger voice and representation in decision-making at all levels. In this context, they welcomed the suggestion for enhanced participation of developing countries in the Financial Stability Forum (FSF).

Both the Commonwealth Finance Ministers and the G-24, at their meeting in Prague in September 2000, were encouraged by recent modifications in the IMF's Contingent Credit Line (CCL) which simplified its review procedure, increased the amount of resources that can be released without additional conditionality and lowered its cost. Commonwealth Finance Ministers further emphasised that the Fund's credibility as the principal crisis manager in the system required that it should have access to sufficient resources. The G-24 went further, calling for the study of a systemic emergency facility that could decisively underpin confidence in the face of severe market crises; this facility could be funded through the temporary creation of Special Drawing Rights (SDRs), which could be withdrawn when the need for them had passed.

The G-24 also emphasised the traditional responsibility of the IMF to stand ready to support balance of payments adjustment of all its members, including the poorest among them. They also stressed the need for flexibility in Fund facilities to meet the diverse requirements of the Fund's heterogeneous membership, given their different stages of development and the variety of shocks affecting them. The G-24 also emphasised the need for a larger voice for developing economies in the decision-making process of the Fund.

As regards the World Bank, Commonwealth Finance Ministers saw important continuing roles for three of its functions: advice and channelling longer-term concessional assistance (through the International Development Association (IDA)) to low-income countries; a combination of policy advice and non-concessional lending to middle-income countries, complementing private finance; and support for the provision of a range of global public goods. Commonwealth Finance Ministers emphasised that the Bank's role in providing knowledge about development was most effective when combined with finance. In this context, Commonwealth Finance Ministers regarded as disturbing developments the recent decline in the volume of Bank non-concessional lending (especially if crisis-related lending was excluded) and the decline in net IDA lending; they considered that these trends needed to be reversed.

Commonwealth Finance Ministers welcomed the report of the Commonwealth Secretariat/World Bank/IMF joint conference on Developing Countries and the International Financial Architecture and called for the continued collaboration of these institutions in monitoring developments and arranging a second conference in a year's time to take stock of progress achieved in reform of the global system.

The G-24 welcomed the efforts being made by the IMF Managing Director and the World Bank President to move away from micro-management in their conditionalities to emphasise country ownership and to invoke a more participatory approach.

The G-24 Ministers recognised the positive aspects of international standards and codes, noted that participation of developing countries in discussions on the development of these standards and codes has been limited, and called for a more inclusive process. They underlined the voluntary nature of the implementation of such codes and standards, taking into account countries' institutional capacities and stages of development. Echoing the analysis made at the joint Conference, the G-24 meeting stressed the highly asymmetric application of codes and standards. Standards in the area of transparency are pressed on developing countries without corresponding obligations for disclosure by financial institutions, including highly-leveraged institutions. The G-24 therefore insisted that any monitoring of standards and codes by the Bretton Woods Institutions should be done on a strictly symmetric basis.

The G-20 Finance Ministers and Central Bank Governors emphasised, amongst other important aspects, that emerging market economies should be supported with technical assistance and policy advice in opening their capital accounts in a well-sequenced manner to benefit from international capital flows while minimising potential risks.

This book contains an analytical report of the discussions at the Conference, together with the main background papers. It is intended as a contribution to the important discussion within the international community of reform of the international financial system.

Issues for Discussion

To facilitate and focus discussion at the Conference, key questions for each of the Conference sessions were prepared and distributed in advance.

1. International standards and domestic regulation

The financial crises of the late 1990s underscored the importance of having in place a well-designed national financial framework which can both regulate the private financial sector, and reduce the need for public sector action at times of crisis and the associated costs. This shift in emphasis – from crisis resolution to crisis prevention and mitigation – has led to an agenda in which risk management and strengthening market underpinnings at the national level represent two important complementary aspects.

In this regard, the development and implementation of international standards represents an important aspect of the ongoing international effort to assist countries in addressing the challenges posed by increasing global integration. To be effective, however, standards need to be implemented and observed. The appropriate standards and implementation strategy will vary depending on the stage of development and policy objectives of each country. Therefore, standards should be assessed with respect to their effectiveness and in the context of a country's development strategy

Over the past three years, the international community has made good progress in developing and implementing standards. The standard-setting bodies and the IFIs have put forward a variety of standards, and are in various stages of developing detailed methodologies for assessing how far they are being observed. The World Bank/IMF experimental Reports on Observance of Standards and Codes (ROSCs) provide an organising framework for conducting these assessments, including the evidence drawn from the assessments conducted through the Bank/Fund Financial Sector Assessment Program (FSAP).

Questions

◆ What role can standards play in strengthening economic and financial systems in developing countries? What other steps are needed to strengthen policy-making and financial systems?

◆ Which standards are most important in this regard? Those being assessed by the Bank/Fund in their experimental reports on observance? The 12 standards proposed by the FSF? How should these standards be applied to developing country circumstances?

◆ What are the constraints that developing countries face in implementing international standards? What steps are needed (including technical assistance) to ensure that developing countries move towards observance of internationally recognised standards?

◆ What role should the official sector play in encouraging the adoption of standards?

◆ Should market incentives be used to encourage the adoption of standards? Or is this premature, given the limited experience with them which could give misleading signals to the market?

As noted by the FSF taskforce on implementation of standards, the experience gained through these efforts points to three key factors for fostering implementation of standards: (a) promoting country *ownership*; (b) providing a judicious blend of market and official *incentives*; and (c) mobilising *resources*, both nationally and internationally, through enhanced partnerships.

The taskforce has also proposed a five-stage strategy for the implementation of standards: (a) identifying and forging international consensus on key standards; (b) prioritising standards for implementation, taking into account country circumstances; (c) designing and effecting an action plan to implement standards; (d) assessing progress in observance of standards on an ongoing basis; and (e) disseminating information on progress in observance of standards.

2. International regulation

Since the East Asian crisis, there has been considerable discussion of the need for, and issues related to, international financial regulation as a complement to the strengthening of domestic financial systems.

One outcome has been the creation of new fora such as the Financial Stability Forum and the G-20 in order to provide additional institutional mechanisms for identification and ongoing discussion of systemic issues. An explicit objective has been to broaden participation, but the inclusion of developing countries in some of the discussions, such as those carried on in the FSF, is still extremely limited.

As regards international regulation, a number of studies and proposals have emerged, including from the FSF Working Groups and the Basle Committee, on subjects such as bank lending, hedge funds, mutual funds and offshore centres, with the aim either of modifying existing regulations or of introducing new measures where gaps exist. As yet there has been relatively limited progress in implementation.

As a result of the Asian and other crises, an interesting new question has arisen as to whether regulation, both national and international, should have explicit counter-cyclical elements in an attempt to compensate for pro-cyclical tendencies in private behaviour.

Questions

◆ What are the best institutional arrangements for international co-operation on systemic issues?

◆ In relation to which actors and sectors should international regulation most urgently be modified or introduced to reduce the likelihood of future crises? What type of measures should be introduced? How would such measures affect both the stability and level of capital flows to developing countries?

◆ Should explicit counter-cyclical elements be introduced into international regulation? How could this best be done?

◆ In what areas is it particularly important, especially for policy-makers in developing countries, to improve timely information on international capital markets? How can this best be achieved?

3. Private sector involvement

The involvement of the private sector is critical to forestall and resolve financial crises; prevention remains the first line of defence against crises. In this regard, several measures have been identified, including the adoption of collective action clauses in sovereign bonds, call options in interbank loans, private sector contingency financing and the setting up of creditor committees.

The most difficult issue remains how to involve the private sector in face of, or in the aftermath of a crisis. The need to secure appropriate private sector involvement now seems reasonably well accepted, including by the private financial community, and the experience with some recent cases has been encouraging.

There is also broad consensus on the underlying principles that were put forward by the G-7. IMF staff have proposed an operational framework based on these principles.

With this approach, private sector involvement could be ensured primarily through reliance on the IMF's traditional catalytic role:

◆ if the member's financing requirements are moderate; or

◆ if the member has good prospects of rapidly regaining market access on appropriate terms, even in cases in which the financing requirements are large.

More concerted forms of private sector involvement could be required:

◆ if the financing requirement is large and the member has poor prospects of regaining market access in the near future; or

◆ if the member has an unsustainable medium-term debt burden.

Although this framework provides a useful start, making it operational requires an assessment of the appropriate means and timing in individual cases and raises difficult analytical and market judgements.

Questions

◆ The IMF has been developing experience with the concerted involvement of the private sector in the resolution of financial crises for two and a half years. Has any success been achieved? Has it damaged the ability of a wide range of emerging market and developing countries to attract private capital?

◆ Would there be merit, as we move forward, in providing greater clarity about the circumstances in which concerted private sector involvement should be required? What should be the role of the IMF in this regard? Should we move towards a more mechanical rule-based system?

◆ Are the tools available to the international community for securing concerted private sector involvement able to handle the wide range of future cases that might arise? If outflows are broad based – and extend beyond a withdrawal of interbank lines from foreign commercial banks and payments in respect of international sovereign bonds – how could concerted private sector involvement be secured? Would there be a case, under certain circumstances, for countries experiencing such outflows to use temporary standstill?

◆ What pre-emptive measures can be taken to reduce the likelihood and costs of private sector-related payment difficulties? What are the views on the recent steps taken by some industrial countries to encourage wider use of collective action clauses? Is this a useful precedent for developing countries to adopt, and are they now more likely to do so?

4. Capital account liberalisation and its critique

Since the East Asian crisis, there has been fairly broad agreement that capital account liberalisation should be very gradual and properly sequenced. Furthermore, there is agreement that liberalisation of potentially more reversible flows should proceed very carefully, and not take place till significant macro-economic imbalances have been reduced and till domestic financial systems are strong and well regulated, so as to help avoid costly currency and banking crises.

Questions

◆ What is the most appropriate pace of liberalisation of the capital account for different categories of countries that have not yet embarked on liberalisation? For example, what is the appropriate pace for small and large countries, for low-income and middle-income countries? Is it advisable and feasible for countries that have significantly liberalised to somewhat reverse this process?

◆ What types of controls are most effective in different country circumstances, in the light of recent experience? What problems arise in their implementation, and how can they be overcome?

◆ Given that countries suffer the effects of crises, and that a new international financial architecture is not yet in place, should developing countries have full autonomy to decide on their capital account liberalisation? How can they best benefit from systematic evaluation on international experience of capital account liberalisation?

◆ What are the linkages between capital controls, lender of last resort and orderly debt work-outs?

5. The role of IFIs in the new architecture

There is a growing consensus that the role of IFIs needs to be adapted to help developing and transition economies meet two major challenges: (a) how to integrate into the world economic and financial system in such a way that they can maximise the benefits of globalisation, while minimising the costs; and (b) how to help developing countries with the broader challenge of development and, especially, poverty reduction. The first challenge implies helping developing countries to attract sufficient sustained private capital flows, whilst strengthening measures for crisis prevention and better crisis management. The second implies supporting policies and structural reforms that facilitate development, and helping countries to secure sufficient external funding, both official and, more especially, private funding, to sustain growth and reduce poverty.

To fulfil, as far as possible, these two major roles, it is important to define: (a) the key tasks that need to be fulfilled by respective IFIs, especially the World Bank and the IMF; (b) the mechanisms to be used (for example, lending facilities); (c) the division of labour among the IFIs, as well as collaborative arrangements; and (d) appropriate governance of the IFIs, including appropriate participation by developing countries. Although there is broad consensus on the overarching objectives that the IFIs have collectively to meet, there has been renewed and intense debate on the specific mandates and division of responsibilities, given the changing global context, and especially the substantial increase and potential volatility of private capital flows.

Questions

◆   What are the main changes in the global context that have a bearing on the role of international institutions? What are the gaps that have been identified in the aftermath of the East Asian crisis? What are the other challenges that international financial institutions need to respond to?

◆   What do these new challenges imply for the role of the international financial institutions, notably the Bank and Fund? What do they suggest for the delineation of responsibilities between the Bank and the Fund? How can we preserve clarity of mandates and accountability, and yet ensure coherence in what is now an increasingly interconnected agenda?

◆   In what ways do instruments of the two institutions need to adapt to changing circumstances? What are the implications for the content, design and co-ordination of conditionality?

◆   What are the implications of this evolving agenda for the modalities of collaboration between the Bank and the Fund, and the involvement of other institutions such as the regional development banks? In what way can regional arrangements complement efforts at the global level?

PART 1
REPORT OF THE CONFERENCE

Developing Countries and the Global Financial System[1]

Stephany Griffith-Jones and Amar Bhattacharya

Introduction

On 22 and 23 June 2000 a major Conference on Developing Countries and the Global Financial System was held in London; it was jointly organised by the Commonwealth Secretariat, the World Bank and the IMF. The Conference brought together senior policy-makers from the International Financial Institutions (IFIs), and from developed and developing countries, as well as private sector representatives and academics. One of the key aims of the Conference was to provide a forum for senior policy-makers from developing countries to define and express their views on the future roles of the IFIs, facilitating a stronger voice for them in this important debate. The results of this Conference have been useful in preparing inputs for the Commonwealth Finance Ministers' Meeting in Malta, and may also be of interest to the next G-20 meeting and the Annual Meetings of the IMF/World Bank.

The following were the main issues discussed:

◆   International standards and domestic regulation

◆   International regulatory challenges

◆   Private sector involvement in crisis resolution

◆   The role of the IFIs in the new financial architecture

◆   Issues of global governance

◆   Capital account liberalisation and its critique.

On all these issues, the aim was to have a candid exchange of views, to try to narrow differences and to explore new technical challenges. One important theme was the future role of the IFIs in the context of the debate that began after the publication of several reports, including that by Meltzer. A summary of the various presentations and discussions at the Conference follows. It does not give full details of all views expressed as the discussion was extremely rich. The list of participants is given in Appendix B.

---

[1]The authors wish to thank Axel Peuker from the World Bank for valuable inputs into this report. Thanks to Ricardo Gottschalk, Stephen Spratt and Xavier Cidera for excellent notes on the meeting.

Overview

Opening the Conference, Dame Veronica Sutherland, Deputy Secretary-General (Economic and Social Affairs), Commonwealth Secretariat noted that the design of a new international financial system was high on the international agenda, as a result of the frequency, severity and high development costs of recent financial crises. She said that what was needed was to identify a new system appropriate for the needs of the twenty-first century.

There had been progress in a number of areas. The lending facilities of the IMF for crisis prevention and management had been usefully expanded and adapted, and there had been some modification of conditionality. Institutional innovations had been introduced, such as the creation of the Financial Stability Forum (FSF), and the creation first of the G-22 and, more recently, of the G-20. A more flexible approach had also been adopted on capital account liberalisation. Developing countries which were recipients of private capital flows had introduced some important measures including, for example, the provision of better information to international financial markets and better regulation and supervision of their domestic financial systems. Other measures were designed to make these countries less vulnerable to currency and financial crises.

Even though the progress made so far on designing a new international financial architecture had been important, it was somewhat asymmetrical. In particular, there were three aspects where a broader approach would be beneficial. The first was the issue of capital flows. Crises such as those in East Asia were caused not just by problems in the East Asian countries themselves, but to a large extent by imperfections in international capital markets, which led to rapid surges and reversals of massive private flows. To deal with the problems of very large and potentially reversible capital flows, there was a clear need for better international regulation of private capital flows. It was also arguable that there was a need for sufficiently large international provision of official liquidity to control crises within countries and to prevent them from spreading to other countries. Progress in these two areas had taken place, although it was fairly limited. The FSF had produced very good working party reports on hedge funds and on off-shore centres, but their recommendations were only now beginning to be implemented and important regulatory gaps continued to exist. The Basle Accord on Capital Adequacy was being revised, but action had yet to be taken to reduce excessive regulatory bias which seemed to encourage short-term bank lending to developing countries.

Broader issues of the further expansion of IMF resources for times of crises needed to be explored, including the possibility raised by Michael

Camdessus, in one of his last speeches as Managing Director of the IMF, of funding a facility like the Contingent Credit Line (CCL) with a temporary creation of Special Drawing Rights (SDRs); these would be self-liquidating as the crises receded and loans were paid back.

A second source of asymmetry in the process of international financial reform had been the limited participation of developing countries, including the main emerging market countries, in the process, especially in the decision-making fora. Clearly the participation of developing countries in the G-22 and now the G-20 was a useful step, though these fora were mainly of a consultative nature. However, it would be a major step forward if developing countries and development concerns were represented in key fora such as the FSF. Indeed, when the FSF was created, it was announced that its membership could be broadened.

A third and final source of asymmetry had been the undue focus on crisis prevention and management, mainly for middle-income countries. Important as this is, it may have led to neglect of the equally, if not more, important issues of appropriate external financing for low-income countries. These required development finance in the form of multilateral lending, official aid and debt relief. They also needed official and other assistance to catalyse more significant private capital flows.

Finally, it was a serious source of concern for developing countries and for all those concerned with development that views were now emerging, mainly from the industrialised countries, for a significant scaling down of lending by the IMF and the World Bank. As several of the papers prepared for the Conference point out, these proposals are exactly the opposite of what developing countries, and indeed the world economy, need. Amongst the crucial roles of the Bretton Woods Institutions were the provision of liquidity and of longer-term development finance. In both cases, the IFIs filled gaps not covered, or not yet covered, by private flows, either because private lenders or investors had temporarily withdrawn or because they were not willing to finance certain countries, sectors or projects.

Not only was it important to reaffirm the value of IFIs in today's and tomorrow's world, it was also crucial to make suggestions on how best to adapt their lending facilities, as well as the conditionality attached to them, so as to maximise the effectiveness of IFIs' contribution to development.

In his opening remarks, Kemal Dervis, Vice-President, Poverty Reduction and Economic Management Network, World Bank, emphasised that in the debate about globalisation and its management the challenge went beyond just economic or financial aspects. The real debate in international finance, as in other areas, was which levels of sovereignty were responsible for what actions?

The Asian crisis had encouraged ongoing discussion on a new financial architecture. There was a risk that the rapid recovery of growth – in the crisis countries and the world economy – could reduce the sense of urgency of this debate.

There were two good and two bad elements associated with globalisation. The two good ones were that overall growth was robust and developing countries were increasingly participating in the process; and that, as recent World Bank studies had confirmed, growth was good for the poor. As a reflection of these developments, human indicators showed massive progress in the last decade. The overall conclusion, therefore, was that globalisation was good for poverty reduction.

The two bad elements, however, were that the severity and frequency of crises had increased over time, and that volatility seemed to be a phenomenon that was here to stay. There were surges of capital flows before World War I, and again in the 1920s and the 1970s, all of which ended with major dislocations in the world economy. Comparatively, the recent crises were not the worst. Given the regularity and high cost of crises, there was an urgent need to continue efforts to reduce such problems.

Secondly, there was a group of the poorest countries which were not benefiting from globalisation; their per capita income had not grown and their share of world trade was falling. They were being left out and this was a major challenge.

As regards the role of the IFIs, the depression of the 1930s and World War II had provided a rationale for the creation of the Bretton Woods Institutions. The Cold War had provided initial justification for aid and multilateral lending. Today, however, aid was justified in terms of poverty reduction.

In the current Heavily Indebted Poor Countries (HIPC) initiative, debt reduction was seen as being linked to growth and poverty-reduction policies. In that context, strategies to be pursued had to be designed by the affected country, but the IFIs' staff had to assess the programmes which would need the approval of the IFIs' boards of directors. In poor countries macro and structural policies were intertwined, and this made close co-operation with the IMF and the World Bank essential. This was also true for middle-income countries. In country programmes, there was a multitude of agencies and actors to be co-ordinated, but ultimately success would depend upon the dynamics of the country itself.

In the debate, a significant point was made that it was important not to overlook the different sizes of developing countries. Though the economies of small countries had been growing, their growth was both more vulnerable and more volatile.

International Standards and Domestic Regulation

There was broad agreement amongst participants about the importance of international standards. The significance of standards for building up sound financial systems and for promoting stability of the international financial system was particularly emphasised. Two key objectives of standards were highlighted: (i) to help policy-makers in developing countries, by providing a benchmark; and (ii) to provide more and better information to markets so that they could price risks more appropriately; this, in turn, would hopefully provide feed-back mechanisms for policy-makers.

The need for standards was caused by several elements. Globalisation meant that countries were increasingly linked, and as a consequence externalities were significantly increased. Indeed, the rapid growth of capital flows, and the increased emphasis on private markets, had speeded up the international transmission of shocks. Recent experience had shown the significance of contagion. In this context, some participants stressed the value of implementing consistent and uniform standards across countries; facilitating comparability of information would hopefully reduce the likelihood of crises and their contagion. Other participants stressed the need for adapting standards to country circumstances.

A number of concerns were expressed by developing country participants about the relevance, scale and nature of standards, and the legitimacy of the process involved in designing them. These concerns were perhaps best summarised in the question of whether standards were a runaway juggernaut or a desirable reform.

As regards the reason why so much emphasis had been placed on implementation of standards by developing countries, the argument was put forward that standards were the lowest common denominator of agreement among key players regarding measures leading to the setting up of a new financial architecture. It was far more difficult to reach agreement on more radical and international measures, such as the various alternatives of 'lender of last resort' and involving the private sector in crisis resolution. This was linked to the fact that implementing standards required little effort from G-7 countries, which were the key decision-makers in the international arena.

A number of general concerns were raised by developing country participants, several of which were widely shared. Firstly, the question was raised as to whether standards could really play such a large role in preventing crises, given the importance of other factors, such as exchange rate policies. Indeed, the fear was expressed that the micro-rationality of standards (especially in the financial sector) could be overwhelmed by the large macro-economic shocks that tended to be important features of crises. The concern was even raised that implementation of standards could distract policy-makers from dealing with the main potential causes of crises. Secondly, it was stressed that the number of standards (more than 60) was clearly excessive and that implementing them simultaneously would be very costly. A call was made for a cost-benefit analysis of different standards. This would allow a prioritisation of core standards. Thirdly, the advocacy of uniform standards assumed that 'one size fits all', and did not allow for the variety of institutional structures in different countries. Fourthly, given the absence of a sound analytical basis, it certainly seemed premature to incorporate standards as part of routine IMF conditionality. Furthermore, the fear was expressed that even if, during surveillance, countries had their standard implementation easily approved, during crises perceived lack of implementation of standards could be an obstacle to obtaining adequate emergency official finance.

Doubts were also expressed about the process of defining standards. Firstly, the question was asked whether the process of definition of standards was legitimate; should standards be set by international organisations, with so little participation by developing countries? Or should there be negotiation about which standards should be complied with? Secondly, the need to involve more of the private sector in both the design and implementation of standards was emphasised, given that the primary motive for standards was to encourage more (and stable) private capital flows.

Important differences between developing countries also emerged on what types of standards they regarded as more appropriate, especially in the financial sector. This led to the question of whether the same Basle capital adequacy standard should be applied to countries in different stages of development and degrees of opening of the capital account. The Basle capital adequacy standard was seen as too high for some developing countries, where banks were especially crucial to financial growth due to the limited development of capital markets, the high cost of raising additional capital and smaller perceived risks of crises due to more limited opening of the capital account. The fear was also expressed that in countries with large unregulated sectors, stringent capital adequacy standards and regulation could lead to an undesirable expansion of unregulated financial institutions. On the other hand, for developing countries with more open capital accounts, a clear need was seen for higher capital adequacy requirements than those specified under the Basle Accord, so as to reduce vulnerability to costly crises in a context of large and volatile capital flows.

Indeed, the high development cost of bank failures was stressed by several participants as an important reason for higher capital adequacy requirements and other prudential measures in developing countries than the minimum required by the Basle Accord. However, the need for more stringent capital adequacy requirements for developing country banks did pose a serious problem in that this would make them less competitive with the large international banks, whose capital adequacy requirements would be lower; this could lead to large international banks displacing developing country banks, which some saw as undesirable. The need to implement cross-border regulation, together with national regulation, was also stressed; this would go beyond the Basle tradition.

There was broad agreement amongst all participants on several important issues. Some standards clearly needed to be given priority over others. There should be adequate transition phases. Standards should be voluntary and, in particular, the timing and sequencing of standards should be left to individual countries. Developing country concerns should be appropriately reflected in the development of standards. For this purpose, it was crucial that developing country representatives should speak out even more than they had done so far in relevant fora, such as the IMF Board and the G-20.

International Regulatory Challenges

In this session there was broad consensus on the diagnosis of problems but some differences were expressed on remedial measures.

A key problem in international financial markets was that because of externalities markets could not price risk efficiently. This required a regulatory structure to deal with market imperfections. For this regulation to be efficient, the regulator needed to cover the whole domain where these externalities occurred. With today's globalised private financial markets, this required global modalities of regulation.

Two key elements had a bearing on these international regulatory challenges, specifically in relation to financial markets in emerging markets. One was the weakness of domestic financial institutions and infrastructure revealed in recent crises; the second was the pressures arising from 'global consolidation', that is, the emergence of internationally fewer and bigger banks, the concentration of securities trading, etc. In the case of banking, consolidation raised questions about the weakening of competition.

Lessons were drawn from recent crises. The most obvious one was that capital flows were volatile; this volatility resulted in large swings in capital movements and/or sizeable changes in asset prices. Small open economies – especially emerging ones – were, and are likely to remain, particularly vulnerable to disruption by large flows of international capital. Unfortunately it seemed that this volatility was not just transitional, as it had persisted through the 1990s; indeed, it was reported that during the 1990s the financial system had been in crisis for 40 out of the 120 months, or for 33 per cent of the time. These crises had a large impact on real economies, especially in developing countries. Volatility was probably intrinsic to modern financial markets, and could arise even in countries that were well-managed. Indeed, market participants (especially in the short run) found it hard to discern between the good and the unsustainable; they would often herd and contagion was common.

As a consequence, it was argued that the process of international financial intermediation had a second-best element, in which welfare for both source and recipient countries could be increased by regulatory changes – in source and/or recipient countries – to reduce excessive lending or investing. Such regulatory changes could help smooth capital flows to emerging markets without discouraging them excessively. There was growing recognition that it may often be desirable to regulate excessive surges of potentially reversible capital flows in recipient emerging countries. However, the experience of the 1990s, with very large movements of international funds compared to the small size of developing country markets, implied a strong case for complementary regulation in the source countries. Indeed, in a second-best world, where there was moral hazard due to likely bail-outs on the lender's side and sovereign risk on the borrower's side, large negative externalities on welfare were generated. The introduction of regulatory measures in both source and recipient countries reduced the risk of defaults and crises, as well as raising welfare in both countries.

On the basis of the above diagnosis, several of the speakers argued for better international financial regulation, though there were some differences on how best to proceed. On one side of the spectrum was the proposal for a World Financial Authority; if this should prove impossible, the assignment of the responsibilities to be performed by such an authority could be allocated to existing institutions. The economic challenges for such an international regulator would be to: (a) keep pace with the rapid changes in markets; (b) develop a theory of regulation, which linked regulation of micro-economic risk to the macro-economic cycle; and (c) harmonise global risk management with different structures in different economies.

Some participants argued for a looser approach, on the grounds that a single global regulator was not practical, given different legal regimes; this approach would imply further developing existing co-operation (especially on information) between regulators, consolidated supervision and technical assistance to non-G-10 countries.

A number of important new technical issues were raised. One was the interaction between herding, risk management and transparency in bank lending which, it was argued, actually made markets more prone to crisis. This was linked to the models used by banks to manage risks, for limiting their daily earnings at risk; when this limit was exceeded, the banks automatically reduced exposure by switching into what they believed were less volatile assets. However, individual banks underestimated the impact on prices, volatility and correlations when many investors herded and sold the same asset at the same time. A key reason why investors and bankers herded was that, in a world of uncertainty, the best way of exploiting the information of others was by copying what they were doing. The problem was that while market participants behaved strategically in relation to one another, the risk models measured risk statically, without taking these strategic interactions into account. In other words, risk models had limited value in measuring exposure to rare extreme market events.

It was further argued that herding behaviour might actually increase if the frequency of dissemination of information increased significantly (for example, if foreign exchange reserves were published daily), as this would further accentuate herding. Furthermore, a paradox was pointed out: if all banks used similar models, these might contribute to volatility and systemic risk. A partial answer to this type of problem was to provide incentives for banks to adopt broad risk management, not relying on models alone; this would include rigorous stress-testing, to take account of extreme events, which may have not occurred recently, but could take place in the future. Such stress tests should make financial institutions more careful and less prone to herding. It was reported that after the Asian crisis financial institutions had increased resources for stress tests.

A second area of concern was how to fill disclosure and regulatory gaps, such as possible regulation of portfolio flows to emerging markets, originating in institutional investors, like mutual funds, with the aim of smoothing flows to help avoid surges and crises. This could perhaps best be achieved by a variable risk-weighted cash requirement for institutional investors; this would vary with emerging market countries' performance.

As regards disclosure, important gaps existed in relation to aggregate exposures of financial institutions, especially highly-leveraged institutions (such as hedge funds) and banks, which should be urgently remedied. Efforts here needed to be accelerated, including by mandatory requirements for disclosure. It was very important for policy-makers to have far better information on markets, in the same way that information provided to markets on countries had been significantly improved. Transparency should not be a one-way street.

Valuable insights emerging from the FSF report on capital flow volatility (the Draghi Report) were discussed. The first was the need to assess risks and exposures created by capital inflows, emphasising foreign currency liquidity risks; this applied not only to government risks, but also to banks. The Draghi Report argued that the liquidity and foreign exchange exposures of banks in some emerging markets could, as an interim measure, be subject to explicit regulation. In particular, banks' gross foreign currency positions might need to be regulated, as banks use foreign currency borrowing to fund domestic loans. Though the banks' net foreign currency exposure may be small (as they 'balance' foreign assets and liabilities), they remain exposed to credit risk from their borrowers' foreign exchange risks. The Draghi Report listed different possibilities for the limitation of banks' liquidity and foreign exchange exposure, such as minimum holdings of liquid foreign assets, tiered by maturity of borrowing and reserve requirements, with or without remuneration, to discourage foreign currency funding.

The rapidly increased market share of foreign banks in several major emerging markets posed new supervisory challenges. Simple regulations seemed to be useful in some emerging markets. But the trend in supervising big international banks was allowing use of their own risk-management procedures (subject to supervisory verification). Concern was also expressed about this trend and whether regulators were not putting too much faith in the markets. Other banks, especially in developing countries, would still be subject to standardised rules. Applying different standards to domestic and foreign banks in the same country was problematic, raising level playing field issues. In the future, these differences may narrow in some developing countries, whose banks, due to their perceived increased sophistication, may also be allowed by regulators to use their own risk models.

Broader questions were also asked about the willingness of foreign banks to lend to small businesses, and about whether foreign banks were more likely to curtail credit in a crisis. Evidence from South Korea seemed to confirm the latter point.

A final issue raised was the need to remove regulatory distortions, such as those in the 1988 Basle Accord, that may have contributed to the build-up of short-term international debt, due to lower capital adequacy requirements for short-term lending. Rating agencies were also critically assessed, given their pro-cyclical impact; their possible increased role in the proposed new Basle Accord regulations was a source of concern.

The view was expressed that a broader response to pro-cyclical trends in lending itself, and even in regulation, could be the implementation of explicit counter-cyclical elements in bank regulation, to help smooth capital flows and their impact on the domestic financial system, as well as on the real economy. This would better link micro-economic risks, that regulators had, until recently, focused on, and macro-economic risks. Different mechanisms could be used for such counter-cyclical regulation of banks: variable capital ratios, higher general provisions for possible loan losses built up in good times to be used in bad times, caps for the value of collateral in times of boom, and/or discouragement of categories of lending – such as for property or personal consumption – that increased more in booms. Furthermore, regulators should be flexible in the down-turn, particularly to allow banks to cushion themselves in times of recession, even possibly allowing ratios to fall below normally required levels, to help sustain lending. Tension may arise between regulatory concerns about individual banks and macro-externalities of such actions. Further analysis is required about practical issues on the best timing and mechanisms to implement counter-cyclical regulatory measures, and whether such measures should be introduced nationally, internationally, or both.

Private Sector Involvement in Crisis Resolution

There was broad consensus on some issues on private sector involvement at a general level. All actors, including the private sector, had accepted the need for collective action and the idea of their own involvement in crises. There was, especially, consensus on the need for collective action clauses in bonds. Furthermore, there had been significant progress in understanding the issues, but far less progress on implementation. This was partly because the issues were rather complex, but also because there were fairly important differences between the different actors involved on what were the best modalities to use.

It was stressed that private sector involvement encompassed several stages. The first, and most important, was crisis prevention. If prevention was managed correctly, there would be no need for crisis management. A key element in prevention was liquidity risk management, for banks, corporates and the government. Private sector contingent credit lines could also play a positive role here. The other two stages occurred during a crisis. At one level, there could be market disruption without default. Agreements were voluntary, and there was differential treatment for creditors. If this second stage was not successful, the country entered a potential default stage, where reactions were involuntary. The decision involved was crucial for the country which would bear very severe costs; developing country participants expressed the view that the decision should be left to the country and that the IMF should not be involved. Furthermore, the intervention of the Fund at this stage could weaken its future influence. In this stage, debtors seemed to prefer a more rule-based, mechanical procedure, and one in which all creditors should be equally treated. It was argued that the negotiations should be left to creditors and debtors, as this would allow for a faster solution.

The exchange rate regime was stressed as crucial, because it determined the burden-sharing between domestic currency denominated debt and foreign currency denominated debt. More broadly, according to some participants, certain exchange rate regimes (such as floating or very strong pegs) could reduce the probability of crises.

From an IMF perspective, it was also stressed that the Fund should not try to become a party in the negotiations. However, the Fund's analysis of debt sustainability in the medium term should be the basis for discussion. Broadly, the Fund distinguished two situations. In one it would rely on its traditional catalytic approach. This was when the finance problem of the country was moderate, could be sorted out with limited official finance and the country had good prospects of recovering market access. The second situation was the one that required private sector involvement. This was when the financial requirement was large and the country had no prospect of re-accessing the capital markets or, if it had, there was an unsustainable medium-term debt burden.

Generally a criterion could be that if funds required exceeded a certain percentage of the country's IMF quota, then private sector involvement would be required. However, from the IMF perspective, moving towards mechanical rules was seen as problematic, because of the complexity of individual cases; this differed from developing country positions, which preferred a more rule-based approach. Emphasis was put on the difficulty of knowing *ex ante* if the situation would go into a crisis, as information was scarce when markets were disturbed.

The decision on whether or not to involve the private sector needed to be based on a cost-benefit analysis. The main benefits of involvement were: (a) relative predictability of rules; and (b) limiting the risk of large-scale official lending that allowed the private sector to exit and created moral hazard. The main costs were: (a) an adverse effect on prospects of resumption of spontaneous market access by the country concerned; and (b) the range of undesirable effects on international capital markets.

The decision for concerted action depended on the expectation of success; the better the instruments the more likely a positive solution.

The private sector representatives stressed that, from the perspective of the private sector, the framework for involvement should be voluntary, transparent and without a fixed set of rules. Comparability of treatment, better information on burden-sharing, as well as respect for bond-holder majority votes, were stressed as desirable features. It was seen as important to avoid situations where investors feared purchasing bonds; indeed, from the private sector's perspective, the optimum situation was one where debt was very difficult (but not impossible) to restructure and the mechanism was pre-established and not arbitrary.

From a private sector perspective, there were three main principles to be followed by the IMF in its involvement in debt restructuring and crisis management: (a) acceptance of free negotiations for restructuring; (b) verifying that countries really did need debt restructuring; and (c) consultation first with the private sector to assess the magnitude of the problem.

It was emphasised that investors and countries both benefited from quick solutions to crises. For the lender, the longer the default, the lower the recovery rate; for the borrower, unresolved debt claims precluded further access to capital markets.

In relation to criteria for private sector involvement, some participants argued for three elements to be considered: (i) whether the crisis was national or systemic; (ii) whether the crisis was one of liquidity or of solvency (it was, however noted that the distinction between illiquidity and insolvency was difficult in practice); and (iii) in the case of illiquidity, whether official lenders had enough resources to meet the outflows without private sector adjustment. If a crisis was clearly systemic, official money should be provided and the private sector should be involved. The case of national crises is more complicated, as there was a trade-off between the cost of the crisis for the country concerned and moral hazard for the lenders; however, a bias towards lending was seen as desirable. As regards a national crisis, a clear criterion for establishing whether it was a liquidity crisis was whether governments could pay back once the panic was over; if this was the case – as in countries like Mexico in 1995 or Korea in 1997 – then it seemed clearly to be a liquidity crisis. In genuine cases of insolvency, new lending by official creditors should only be made on condition that agreement on a write down of debts was also achieved. Collective action clauses could help ensure this.

The issue of standstills was also discussed. South Korea in 1997 was seen as a successful case of a voluntary standstill, once it was implemented (though the delay in implementing it had led to large bank outflows which deepened the crisis); however, the success of the Korean standstill may be partly explained by the fact that banks were the main creditors, which was not the case in other countries, where creditors were more heterogeneous (for example, bond-holders). As regards unilateral standstills, the question was raised about how comprehensive such a measure should be, and whether it could effectively deter capital flight by residents in an open economy. Indeed, it was argued that standstills needed to be combined with capital controls to make them effective and to prevent capital flight undermining the effectiveness of the standstills.

The Role of the IFIs in the New Financial Architecture

The main themes emerging from this discussion were as follows.

The changing global environment posed a double challenge of crisis mitigation and inclusion of developing countries in the globalisation process. Globalisation had led to increasing growth for selected developing countries, but also to greater vulnerability, stemming increasingly from capital rather than trade shocks, which tended to be dramatic relative to GDP. Information asymmetries increased the risk of herd behaviour by investors and contagion affecting middle-income countries. At the same time, least developed countries had been virtually excluded from the benefits of globalisation, and the number of poor in the world continued to rise. This posed a double challenge: (i) to prevent and mitigate crises in middle-income countries; as well as (ii) to ensure that the poorest and currently excluded countries were not left behind, and that global targets on poverty reduction could be met.

The principal recommendations of the Meltzer Commission, however, did not help the IMF and World Bank to better address these challenges. The discussants unanimously rejected the emphasis of the Meltzer Commission on 'moral hazard' issues in defining the role of the Fund, the assumption that access to private capital flows eliminated any role for the World Bank in middle-income countries and the confidence that the donor community would mobilise sufficient financing to replace IDA loans with grants in low-income countries. Accordingly, they did not think that the Meltzer Commission Report provided an adequate blueprint to guide Bank/Fund reform. The IFIs should continue to pursue the aims for which they were created – supporting stability, growth and development – but they should adapt to the needs of the twenty-first century. Equitable income distribution was also an important policy objective.

Bank/Fund collaboration needed to be improved and strengthened, but there could be no simple delineation of roles and responsibilities in an increasingly complex environment. The two institutions needed to work flexibly together – with each acting as the lead institution on different issues. However, the goal should not be to set artificial boundaries or eliminate any 'overlap' in the work programme of the two institutions. There were important synergies which could only be realised if both institutions retained capacity in critical areas. This applied in particular to the nexus of growth-oriented policies, financial sector development and structural reforms in support of poverty alleviation. This was illustrated by recent initiatives such as enhanced collaboration in crisis countries, Poverty Reduction Strategy Papers (PRSPs), Reports on Observance of Standards and Codes (ROSCs), and Financial Sector Assessment Programmes (FSAPs).

The Fund needed to avoid mission creep, but it needed to retain its facilities for low-income countries. In this context, Fund representatives stressed that the naming of the Poverty Reduction and Growth Facility (PRGF) should not be misinterpreted as an attempt to broaden the Fund's mandate. At the same time, Fund approaches needed to reflect the insight from the Asian crisis that a narrow focus on macro-fundamentals without regard to structural, social and institutional factors was inadequate. There was also strong support for retaining the Fund's facilities for low-income countries, especially to provide liquidity and evoke the discipline which was associated with the combination of surveillance and lending. It was seen as appropriate that the PRGF remained in the Fund, as any change would risk losing already approved resources, and because stabilisation was an essential element of growth and poverty reduction, but continued collaboration with the Bank was desirable.

The Bank had an important role to play in middle-income countries. Access to private capital markets was not a sufficient criterion for withdrawal of Bank support, as countries might not be able to raise necessary finance in the markets, especially for longer maturities and for activities where social returns were higher than market returns. In addition, Bank lending provided stable, counter-cyclical access to funds. It could improve asset-liability management by extending duration, and play an important role as a catalyst for private lending, in particular for capital-intensive investments with long gestation and pay-off terms. In support of policy dialogue, it could also have an important impact on expenditure composition to the benefit of the poor. Bank lending added special value due to its technical contribution. Finally, while discussants expressed concern about the use of Bank resources in crisis situations, it was also acknowledged that the availability of timely and adequate crisis lending could have important development pay-offs (for example, in helping to support social safety nets or helping to strengthen banking systems, when they were under extreme pressure).

It was still felt, however, that the Bank lacked focus and efficiency. In the perception of most discussants, the welcome emphasis by the Bank on dialogue with all stakeholders had unfortunately resulted in an unwarranted effort to be 'all things to all people'. Efficiency had suffered as competencies and resources were stretched thin. In particular, there was an apparent disconnection between initiatives supported by senior management and operational priorities at the country level, with country units frequently complaining about a multitude of 'unfunded mandates'. At the same time, from a client's perspective, desirable safeguard policies tended to translate into administrative hurdles for project approval, further increasing already lengthy preparation cycles. Finally, discussants expressed concern that programming of staff time had created perverse incentives (for example frequent over-commitments), effectively reducing management's ability to mobilise staff. To summarise, although there was extremely strong support for the World Bank's mission, there was a lot of criticism of how the Bank implemented it.

The World Bank still needed to play its original role in financing projects crucial for development in health, education and transport. In particular, but not only from a low-income country perspective, the World Bank should not give up on its role of lending for traditional projects.

In defining its mission, the World Bank should recognise that it did not necessarily have a comparative advantage in the provision of all global public goods. The Bank had an important role to play in the provision of global public goods. However, as was imperative in Bank/Fund collaboration, the Bank should increase its efforts to co-ordinate with other global and regional organisations. In many instances, other global organisations appeared to have a comparative advantage and should take the lead in facilitating the provision of global public goods. Moreover, there often were distinct regional externalities which suggested a critical responsibility of regional organisations; regional institutions may also respond better to the needs of smaller countries.

There remained a tension between conditionality and ownership. There was broad consensus that successful policy reform required country ownership of programmes, and genuine partnerships between countries and IFIs. Nonetheless, some participants underlined the usefulness of conditionality to focus policy dialogue and to express government commitment. However, other discussants voiced concern about the legitimacy of conditionality, which at times still appeared to replace, rather than reflect, government ownership, and thus raised issues of democratic legitimacy and accountability. The view was also expressed that there had been an excessive expansion of conditionality, especially linked to HIPC debt relief. Greater humility by the IFIs was also to be encouraged.

Reforms of Bank/Fund governance would strengthen effectiveness and legitimacy. There was a widespread perception that current arrangements in the international financial architecture did not provide sufficient voice for developing countries (see below). This was also deemed to apply to the governance structure of the Bank and the Fund. Even within the parameters of capital-based representation, the current arrangements in establishing the Board of Directors (with, for example, grouping of OECD and developing countries under one chair, or alphabet-based rotation of shared seats for developing countries) were deemed inadequate. More-over, there was strong support for further focusing the role of the respec-tive Boards on issues of strategic importance, and enhancing the 'deliber-ative' nature of these bodies – a shift which should be reflected in the stature and mandate of Board representatives.

The meeting provided evidence that the discussions on the role of Bank and Fund were beginning to yield concrete results, and that a variety of reform proposals were emerging which were not confined by the ideo-logical underpinnings of the Meltzer Commission. For the Bank, these included (as well as those mentioned above):

◆ strengthening the Bank's role in support of trade liberalisation;

◆ enhancing the capacity of developing countries to conduct WTO negotiations;

◆ rebuilding sectoral competency;

◆ enhancing Bank/International Finance Corporation collaboration.

On a more conceptual level, there was also a discussion about the division of labour between global, regional (and national) development agencies, and a vision of their collaboration in a multi-level network where regional agencies were not just perceived as a replica of global institutions.

Issues of Global Governance

Global governance had resurfaced as a major issue as a result of the Asian crisis. The view was presented that it was desirable that governance of institutions should be discussed in parallel with a redefinition of the func-tions of institutions.

In the depths of the last crisis (around September 1998) calls began to be made by the G-7 for 'reform of the global financial architecture'. The discussions at the Conference focused on whether the progress made had been sufficient to help prevent and respond better to future crises and make them far less damaging and whether the reform process and, more generally, global governance had been inclusive enough.

The view was expressed by several participants that progress on reform had moved in the right direction, but had suffered from two linked problems. Firstly, progress made, though important and clearly valuable, was insufficient, given the magnitude of the changes required; there was the risk that complacency could set in, as the global economy and the crisis-hit countries had recovered so well. Secondly, progress had been asymmetrical. Though significant and useful efforts had been, and were being, made to ensure institutional reforms at the national level in developing countries, it was argued that insufficient progress had been made in the area of international reform. The latter should include provision of adequate official emergency financing, possibly funded by anti-cyclical issues of SDRs to countries experiencing crisis, to be extinguished as they were repaid. It should also include some mechanism for 'standstill' provision to be incorporated into international lending, as well as for strengthening regional and sub-regional organisations so that they could play a greater role in preventing and managing crises. The role of regional institutions was debated but was seen as particularly valuable for smaller countries; it also contributed to valuable diversity of ideas, relevant in a pluralistic world.

As regards the representation of developing countries in global governance and, specifically, in the reform process itself, some positive steps had been taken, but a number of participants saw them as insufficient. The two new vehicles crafted by the G-7 in 1999 to take the reform process forward were the FSF and the G-20; they had now become important actors in the process of international financial reform. Though the creation of the FSF was seen as valuable, concern was expressed that, until now, the FSF had not included developing countries as formal members of the Forum; their inclusion in working groups was not enough. The view was expressed that although the work of the FSF was very valuable, more of its efforts seemed to be geared towards reducing the vulnerability of countries to increasing volatility in the capital markets, rather than influencing the behaviour of the international market actors who played a large role in generating the problem.

In contrast to the mainly G-7 FSF, the G-20 comprised different categories of countries, including major developing ones; this was a welcome feature. However, the absence of smaller countries was noted. The focus of G-20 work was seen as rather narrow. Indeed, the prevailing focus of the G-20 was far more on addressing developing countries' domestic vulnerability to financial crises, rather than the broader international issue of how to reform the global financial architecture.

The view was expressed that the G-20 had so far acted more as a sounding-board for reforms endorsed by the G-7. However, the G-20 was still in its infancy, and the possibility existed of a broadening of its agenda, for example through initiatives taken by non-G-7 members. The statement by the Canadian Finance Minister, Paul Martin, the G-20's first Chairman, was highly encouraging. He said: 'There is virtually no major aspect of the global economy or international financial system that will be outside of the group's purview.' One area suggested for discussion in the G-20 was the role of the IFIs.

Capital Account Liberalisation and its Critique

After the Asian crisis the international consensus moved towards far greater caution on liberalisation of the capital account. This was based on the well-recognised view that although global capital flows had a potential for improving efficiency and growth prospects, especially through the development and deepening of national financial markets, they could also trigger very significant instability, which was particularly costly and painful for developing countries, especially the poorer ones. As a consequence, capital account liberalisation had to be actively managed by national authorities, continuously assessing the costs and benefits of liberalisation vis-à-vis controls or regulation. There was also a broad consensus that such liberalisation, though desirable, needed to be gradual and well-sequenced.

Both external and internal factors were needed to influence the pace and order of liberalisation. Progress on an effective international financial architecture (relating to global arrangements for preventing crises as well as provision of rapid and sufficient official international liquidity and adequate arrangements for burden-sharing) was a major factor determining the desirable pace and sequencing of countries' capital account liberalisation.

As regards the management of the capital account, flexibility in the liberalisation of the capital account, depending on domestic and international developments, was stressed. Some participants argued for a permanent system of controls that could be strengthened or loosened throughout the business cycle, as controls created only in a crisis might be less effective due to the non-existence of institutional mechanisms for putting them into practice.

Several participants stressed the need (even in the liberalised framework of the capital account) to retain an option for the re-imposition of controls, given the fact that capital account liberalisation may have proceeded too fast. Indeed, should the IMF not, for example, recommend to countries which have fully liberalised, and which receive large surges of inflows, that they use Chilean-style capital controls or other measures to discourage these large inflows? It was reported that the IMF has not yet done so, partly due to concerns over the market impact of such a step.

A number of linkages between different policies was stressed. For example, some restrictions on the current account may be needed during transition to a liberalised capital account, to avoid leakages. Capital controls should never be a substitute for an appropriate exchange rate and were ineffective if the exchange rate was unrealistic.

The complex issue of optimal levels of foreign exchange reserves in the new context of large and volatile capital flows was also discussed, with emphasis on the need for significant additional foreign exchange reserves to allow not only for covering current account needs and maturing debt, but also possible reversals of flows, such as portfolio capital and potential domestic capital flight. High forex reserves had the virtue of diminishing risks of crises, but implied significant high net costs.

The linkages between prudent domestic regulation and capital account liberalisation were stressed. Whilst borrowing in foreign markets created forex mismatch, borrowing domestically could lead to maturity mismatches. Indeed, countries like India were able to avoid the Asian type crisis facilitated not only by a relatively closed capital account, but also because of a good regulatory framework of the domestic financial system.

As regards types of capital controls, a distinction was made between price-based and quantitative controls. As regards the former, the Chilean experience indicated that price-based measures could be clearly effective in improving the maturity structure of the debt; there was also empirical evidence that, in Chile, unremunerated reserve requirements provided greater autonomy for monetary policy. Indeed, they helped slow down excessive capital inflows in a time of major surges, which led to less rapid growth of private domestic expenditure and of current account deficit.

Price-based controls were also seen to be better, as they were market-based and non-discriminatory. However, if adequate institutional back-up was not available, it might be necessary to use quantitative controls.

A number of central issues were raised. Was a closed capital account a deterrent to needed reforms? Did it reduce growth? Did it discourage desirable capital flows? The Chinese experience suggested that a closed capital account was not a deterrent to broader reforms and that it could be consistent with very rapid growth. However, it was pointed out by some participants that China, as well as India, were countries with particularly large domestic markets, so that they were not necessarily replicable. But there seemed to be broad agreement that a closed capital account did not discourage desirable capital inflows, as demonstrated by the Chinese experience with very high foreign direct investment. 'Having a door in your house does not imply you are a hermit.'

Several participants stressed that liberalisation of the capital account could aid the process of development and the deepening of national financial and debt markets.

Conclusions

Given the range of views expressed, it was difficult to draw simple conclusions. However, a number of areas of consensus could be discerned. As regards standards, it was seen as urgent to prioritise them, so that countries were not excessively overburdened. The possibility of a negotiated agreement between IFIs and developing countries was emphasised.

Domestic financial regulation was important; however, if large macroeconomic shocks occurred, as happened in the lead-up to or during crises, micro-standards of regulation might not be sufficient to help the financial system to withstand such shocks.

Private sector involvement was broadly accepted. Emphasis was placed on the need for countries to decide standstills. There was a need to clarify what sort of transactions would be subjected to standstills and whether such measures had to be accompanied by capital controls.

As regards the role of IFIs, there had been too much emphasis in the architecture discussions on preventive issues; more emphasis should be placed on their role in crisis management.

The issue of development finance for small and poor countries had also not been sufficiently addressed in current debates. In this context the importance of regional institutions was highlighted.

It was important to define changes in governance of the IFIs simultaneously with any changes to their role, and not, as some argued, afterwards.

A key point was that the IFIs should return to basics. However, this should not imply, as the majority Meltzer Report had argued, a decrease of moral hazard, but rather putting financial stability and, above all, growth and development, as the key objectives of the IFIs. The latter would be consistent with the aims with which the IFIs were created at Bretton Woods.

Finally, the agenda of reform of the IFIs and of the financial system would be here for some time. It would be important for developing countries to participate systematically in this process.

PART 2
PAPERS PRESENTED
AT THE CONFERENCE

New International Standards for Financial Stability: Desirable Regulatory Reform or a Runaway Juggernaut?

Shankar Acharya[1]

This paper briefly reviews the what, why, who and when of standards, discusses some of the motivational origins of the current impetus for standards, summarises the author's understanding of the official Indian view of standards, raises some doubts and issues for discussion, and ends with some concluding remarks.

What, Why, Who and When of Standards

What are standards? Perhaps the best concise description comes from the relevant page of the Financial Stability Forum (FSF)'s website:

Standards are codes, guidelines or principles that set out what are widely accepted good practices. Standards relevant for domestic and international financial systems cover a broad range of areas:

◆ *transparency of fiscal, monetary and financial policies;*

◆ *dissemination of economic and financial data;*

◆ *regulation and supervision of banking securities and insurance;*

◆ *information disclosure, transparency, risk management and internal controls of financial institutions;*

◆ *corporate governance, accounting, auditing and bankruptcy;*

◆ *payment and settlement systems.*

For those who want more details, exploration of the FSF website is a recommended activity.

Why are standards important? According to the FSF website:

---

[1]At the time of the Conference (June 2000) the author was Visiting Research Fellow at Merton College, Oxford University, on leave from regular assignment as Chief Economic Adviser, Ministry of Finance, Government of India. This paper was written in a personal capacity and the views expressed may not be attributed to the Government of India.

The widespread adoption of high-quality internationally accepted standards, or codes of good practice, can make an important contribution to effective policy-making, well-functioning financial markets and a stronger international financial system.[1]

Who sets standards? The FSF lists a number of organisations, including the IMF, the Basle Committee on Banking Supervision (BCBS), the International Organisation of Securities Commissions (IOSCO), the International Association of Insurance Supervisors (IAIS), the Committee on Payment and Settlement Systems (CPSS) and the Organisation for Economic Co-operation and Development (OECD).

When do standards become operational? There is no simple answer to this question. In the case of some standards, such as the Special Data Dissemination Standard (SDDS), a large number of countries (including many developing countries) have already made their prior commitments operational. In the case of others, many countries have accepted standards in principle without committing themselves to deadlines for their attainment. As a rule of thumb, most OECD countries are in compliance (or are close to compliance) with most standards, while many developing countries are at varying distances from compliance with regard to most standards. This is not surprising since financial development (including of institutions and standards) is closely correlated with overall development. One would expect a country like Belgium to be much closer to full compliance on the entire range of standards than a country like Rwanda!

The Recent Resurgence of Standards

Standards have been around for a long time, for example, the Basle prudential norms for the banking sector. Work on some standards, such as those for data dissemination and fiscal transparency, predate the onset of the East Asian crisis in mid-1997. There is no question but that the crisis and its various diagnoses imparted a strong impetus to the design, proliferation and implementation of standards. The IMF, the Bank for International Settlements (BIS) and the newly established FSF have become the nodal institutions for the resurgence of activity relating to standards.

There are several reasons for this resurgence. First, and most obviously, some analysts and policy-makers (especially in some G-7 countries) believe that more and uniformly implemented standards can provide a panacea for prevention of financial crises. For example, Eichengreen, a normally sober analyst of international economics, makes a passionate

---

[1] For more details, see Annex.

plea for stronger standards, strongly implemented:[1]

A first area requiring a major international initiative is international financial standards. In a world of integrated financial markets, international financial stability is impossible without domestic financial stability. Stabilising the financial system consequently requires institutional reforms extending well beyond policies towards external trade and payments. That it requires rigorous disclosure requirements and effective supervision of banks and corporations borrowing on financial markets is now agreed on. Some will argue that this is as far as the international community and the IMF should go in intruding into the internal affairs of countries. I argue that they must in fact go further . . . that the need for domestic institutional reforms with implications for the stability of the international financial markets extends beyond this point. It extends to the use of internationally recognised auditing and accounting practices so that lenders can accurately assess the financial condition of the banks and corporations to which they lend. It extends to effective creditor rights, so that claimants can monitor and control the economic and financial decisions of managers. It extends to investor protection laws to prevent insider trading market cornering, and related practices in whose absence securities markets will not develop. It extends to fair and expeditious corporate bankruptcy procedures, without which debt problems can cascade from borrower to borrower. While these are problems for individual countries to address as they see fit whether they arrive at an adequate solution is also of pressing concern to the international policy community, given the scope for financial problems to spill contagiously across borders.

This paper will put forward some reservations about the 'intrusive' reform agenda outlined above. First it will outline some further reasons for the current preoccupation with standards.

Standards are the lowest common denominator of agreement among key players (notably the G-7 and the IMF) regarding measures for restructuring the pre-Asian-crisis international financial architecture. While there has been a great deal of discussion of more radical suggestions, including restructuring the Bretton Woods Institutions (mooted by the British Government in the early stages of the Asian crisis), incorporating various alternatives of the 'lender of last resort' idea into the international architecture, various schemes for involving the private sector in crisis resolution and so on, the discussion has not yet yielded concrete results. Against such a background, the drive for standards might be responding

---

[1]See Barry Eichengreen, *Towards a New International Financial Architecture*. Institute for International Economics, February 1999, p. 10.

to a thought chain of the following kind: there has been an international financial crisis; we (the 'international community') must do something; standards is something; let's do standards!

A third and related reason could be that implementing international financial standards by and large entails little fresh effort by the G-7 or OECD economies, which are the key decision-making countries in the international economic arena. So the burden of fresh effort involved in the new reforms is cast not on the key decision-makers, but on the rest of the (mostly developing) world. Fourthly, the impetus for standards might have drawn strength from the winds of 'glasnost' that have been blowing through the political and economic affairs of nations in the last 15 years, placing a greater premium on transparency and rules, and putting a discount on discretionary decision-making and opacity.

Standards: The Official Indian View

One interpretation of the official Indian view (the author's understanding is handicapped by ten weeks of absence from official corridors) may be summarised as follows:

◆ Agreement on international financial standards and commitment to progressive moves towards their attainment are a necessary entry price for India's policy of increasing integration into the world economy, including granting a greater role to foreign capital;

◆ Such moves are also impelled by an autonomous desire to reform the domestic financial sector and a growing commitment to greater transparency in economic and financial policies;

◆ Accordingly, India has established a Standing Committee on International Financial Standards and Codes, chaired by Reserve Bank Deputy Governor, Dr. Y. V. Reddy (one of the participants at this conference), which, in turn, has set up ten advisory groups with a general mandate to compare existing Indian practices with prevailing international standards and to make broad recommendations on strategies for bringing about greater convergence. These groups relate to the following subjects:

  – transparency of monetary and financial policies
  – corporate governance
  – payment and settlement systems
  – bankruptcy laws
  – data dissemination
  – insurance regulation
  – banking supervision

– securities market regulation
– fiscal transparency
– accounting and auditing

Clearly it is a serious enterprise.

At the same time, in various international fora such as the IMF and G-20, India has cautioned against inappropriate and untimely use of standards in international economic affairs. Specifically, India has:

◆　argued against a mechanical checklist approach to standards;

◆　strongly emphasised the importance of adequate and flexible transi-tion periods for the attainment of standards, with due allowance for initial country conditions;

◆　expressed opposition to the deployment of standards in IMF condi-tionality.

◆　counselled in favour of identifying priorities in standard setting.

Having stated one view of the official Indian position (subject to suitable correction by Dr. Reddy), this paper will move on to raise some issues and doubts about the general enterprise of international financial standards.

Some Issues

At a general level, standards are clearly desirable – like motherhood and apple pie (at least in the old days!). Nevertheless, taking a cue from Amartya Sen's Harvard Commencement Address, delivered a fortnight ago and entitled 'Global Doubt', the paper will raise a few issues from a developing country perspective.

Firstly, the presumed importance of international financial standards in crisis prevention (as presumed, for example, by Eichengreen in the pas-sage quoted earlier) may be exaggerated. Analysis of major recent finan-cial crises, such as the (EU) Exchange Rate Mechanism crisis of 1992, the Mexican crisis of 1994 and the more recent East Asian crisis, suggests important causal roles for inappropriate exchange rate policy, excessive reliance on short-term external borrowing, high current account deficits in the balance of payments and premature adoption of capital account convertibility, to list just a few of the other important factors frequently cited in analyses of these crises. Hence, from the vantage point of crisis prevention, excessive preoccupation with improving financial standards could detract from adequate attention to other policy factors which are possibly at least as important as financial standards in explaining such crises.

Secondly, the importance of sound financial standards in crisis prevention probably varies with the degree of convertibility on capital account practised by a country. Financial standards in China and India may not have been better than crisis-impacted East Asian countries. But China and India were able to weather the gales of contagion at least partly because of their limited degree of openness on the capital account. Nor is full capital account convertibility an indubitably significant prerequisite for sustained economic development – both economic history and economic analysis demonstrate this.[1] Therefore, hurrying all developing countries down the path of rapid attainment of a uniform set of international financial standards may not be an analytically sound strategy.

Thirdly, the advocacy of uniform standards assumes 'one size fits all'. Surely some elements of the recommended standards (for example, those relating to bankruptcy laws and corporate governance) might be expected to differ considerably to reflect a variety of institutional structures present in different countries.

Fourthly, all this might not have mattered if attainment of the recommended international financial standards was a relatively low-cost proposition. If it were, one could argue that quickly strengthening standards was a good insurance against financial crisis. But available evidence suggests that attaining the recommended standards could be a long and arduous process. In that case it is surely relevant to essay some kind of cost-benefit assessment, however heuristic?[2]

Fifthly, in the absence of a sound analytical basis, it is surely premature to advocate, as Eichengreen does, the incorporation of standards as part of routine IMF conditionality. Such conditionality is already often burdened by dubious elements – the addition of a fresh new set of doubtful desired data is probably not called for.

Sixthly, before cheerleading for rapid adoption of uniform standards, there is an urgent need to prioritise and identify core standards. As Andrew Crockett of the BIS notes, there are now over 60 standards on

---

[1] See, for example, Jagdish Bhagwati, 'The Capital Myth: The Difference between Trade in Widgets and Dollars', *Foreign Affairs* 77:7–12,1998 and various papers by Joseph Stiglitz.

[2] The argument that financial crises typically exact tolls amounting to a significant percentage of GDP, and that therefore standards are a good insurance, is not valid in the absence of evidence on either the relative roles of standards versus other factors (such as inappropriate exchange rate policy) in causing crises or the costs of attaining standards.

the website of the FSF![1] Prioritisation would lend greater credence and practicability to the enterprise of bringing in uniform international financial standards. Crockett appreciates the complexity of implementing standards. He states: 'It would be unreasonable to expect an emerging or developing country with a rudimentary financial sector to comply with standards that an advanced financial centre has reached only after decades of development. Sensitivity will be required to balance the desire to move quickly to best practice, with the need to recognise practical constraints.'

Seventhly, there may be greater need to involve the private sector in both the design and implementation of standards than is currently envisaged. We have to remind ourselves (and the standard setters) that a primary motive for having standards is to encourage more (and more orderly) private capital flows. Therefore it would seem reasonable to have greater consultation with the private sector, especially in identifying core standards. Furthermore, when it comes to implementation, it may be much more effective to rely on market incentives and disincentives rather than *dirigiste* tools such as IMF conditionality.

Concluding Remarks

So, returning to the title of this paper, are international financial standards desirable regulatory reforms or are they becoming a runaway juggernaut? This paper has attempted to raise issues and doubts as a warning against the danger of the latter possibility without wholly detracting from the real value of the former.

In answering these questions the following rules of thumb or guidelines should be considered:

◆   International financial standards can play a very useful role in strengthening domestic financial systems and, as a result, the international financial system.

◆   There is a need for prioritisation and identification of core standards. The pace, pattern and intensity of standards implementation should be left to member countries of the international community, with market incentives playing the key role.

◆   The IMF's role should be limited to the dissemination of information; it should not extend to the incorporation of standards into Fund conditionality.

---

[1] Andrew Crockett, 'Progress Towards Greater International Financial Stability'. Mimeo, May 2000.

◆ Above all, standards should not distract countries from the design and management of sensible macro-economic policy, especially with regard to exchange rates, external debt management and the pace of movement towards capital account convertibility.

Annex. Extract from the Financial Stability Forum website

Compendium of Standards

What are Standards?

Standards are codes, guidelines or principles that set out what are widely accepted as good practices. Standards relevant for domestic and international financial systems cover a broad range of areas:

- transparency of fiscal, monetary and financial policies;

- dissemination of economic and financial data;

- regulation and supervision of banking, securities and insurance;

- information disclosure, transparency, risk management and internal controls of financial institutions;

- corporate governance, accounting, auditing and bankruptcy; and

- payment and settlement systems.

Why are Standards Important?

The widespread adoption of high-quality internationally accepted standards, or codes of good practice, can make an important contribution to effective policy-making, well-functioning financial markets and a stronger international financial system.

Enhanced disclosure of economic and financial statistics and greater transparency of the processes by which governments formulate macroeconomic and financial policies will improve the accountability of policy-makers and help markets to adjust more smoothly to economic developments, minimise contagion and reduce volatility. Adopting internationally accepted standards of financial supervision and regulation will help policy-makers implement policies that promote sound and efficient markets and enhance credibility and investor confidence.

Providing market participants with internationally recognised benchmarks on disclosure, transparency, risk management and other practices and procedures against which to compare information, should lead to better informed lending and investment decisions. Transparency of the private sector is of particular importance to the orderly and efficient functioning of financial markets.

Through promoting sound policy-making and orderly and efficient markets, the voluntary adoption of standards of good practice will in turn help to make the international financial system stronger and more stable.

Who are the Standard-Setting Bodies?

International Monetary Fund (IMF): The IMF develops and monitors international standards in areas of direct operational relevance to its mandate to carry out surveillance over the international monetary system. In collaboration with other standard-setting bodies, it has developed international standards for data dissemination and transparency practices in fiscal, monetary and financial policies, and has contributed to the development of international standards for banking supervision. The IMF has prepared on an experimental basis several country reports on implementation of standards and codes of best practices.
http://www.imf.org

Basel Committee on Banking Supervision (BCBS): The BCBS, established by the G10 Central Banks, provides a forum for regular co-operation among its member countries on banking supervisory matters. The BCBS formulates broad supervisory standards and guidelines and recommends statements of best practice in banking in the expectation that bank supervisory authorities will take steps to implement them.
http://www.bis.org

International Organisation of Securities Commissions (IOSCO): IOSCO is an organisation for co-operation among national regulators of securities and futures markets. IOSCO develops and promotes standards of securities regulation in order to maintain efficient and sound markets. It draws on its international membership to establish standards for effective surveillance of international securities markets and provides mutual assistance to promote the integrity of markets by a rigorous application of the standards and effective enforcement against offences.
http://www.iosco.org

International Association of Insurance Supervisors (IAIS): The IAIS, established in 1994, is a forum for co-operation among insurance regulators and supervisors from more than 100 jurisdictions. It is charged with developing internationally endorsed principles and standards that are fundamental to effective insurance regulation and supervision. After having developed the IAIS Core principles, Insurance Concordat and several other standards, much of the IAIS's recent work on standard setting has focused on developing standards in the areas of solvency, insurance concordat to cover cross-border service provision, asset risk management, group co-ordination of financial conglomerates, reinsurance, market conduct and electronic commerce.
http://www.iaisweb.org

Committee on Payment and Settlement Systems (CPSS): The CPSS, established by the G10 Central Banks, provides a forum for regular co-operation among its member central banks on issues related to payment and settlement systems. It monitors and analyses developments in domestic payment, settlement and

clearing systems as well as in cross-border and multi-currency netting schemes. It also provides a means of co-ordinating the oversight functions to be assumed by the G10 Central Banks with respect to these netting schemes. The CPSS formulates broad supervisory standards and guidelines and recommends statements of best practice in banking in the expectation that bank supervisory authorities will take steps to implement them. In addition to addressing general concerns regarding the efficiency and stability of payment, clearing, settlement and related arrangements, the Committee pays attention to the relationships between payment and settlement arrangements, central bank payment and settlement services and the major financial markets which are relevant for the conduct of monetary policy.
http://www.bis.org

Organisation for Economic Cooperation and Development (OECD): The OECD aims to promote policies designed to achieve sustained economic growth and employment in its member countries. In the area of promoting efficient functioning of markets, the OECD encourages the convergence of policies, lawshttp://www.oecd.org

How is the Compendium Organised?

The standards contained in the *Compendium* can be referenced by: (a) the **subject areas** listed below; (b) the **issuing bodies** listed in the previous page; or (c) **date**, by clicking on the relevant links in the horizontal "Browse by" navigation bar above. The subject areas are:
• Public sector;
• Banking;
• Securities;
• Insurance;
• Corporate; and
• Payment and Settlements.

These subject areas are further categorised into relevant sub-sections. The standards are listed under these sub-sections with their full titles and a synoptic description. Each of these standards is in turn linked to a more detailed **data field** which contains the following information:

• Document Name:
• Subject Area:
• Issuing Body:
• Date:
• Status:
• Language:
• Location: *this is a hyperlink to where the source standard is located on the issuing body's website*
• Synoptic Description: 30–50 words
• Detailed Description: 200–1000 words

International Standards and Domestic Regulation

Alastair Clark

Introduction

Standards and codes, in one form or another, have helped to shape the environment for international economic and financial relations for a long time. In some cases these standards and codes have been enshrined in treaties or other formal legal agreements. But in many cases they have not, and whether and, if so, how they have then been implemented has to a significant extent been at the discretion of individual countries.

This paper discusses current initiatives in the area of standards and codes under the headings of 'Why?', 'What?' and 'How?'. Why are these initiatives being pursued? What standards and codes are we talking about? How, in practice, is it proposed that they should be implemented?

Why?

A number of factors have contributed to the recent focus on standards and codes.

First, **globalisation**. National economies are increasingly interlinked, so that problems in one can have rapid and significant knock-on effects in others. Put in a slightly different way, as countries seek to integrate themselves more closely into the global economy, the externalities associated with their conduct of national economic and financial policies increase. Other members of the 'club' may understandably look for reassurance that everyone is playing by broadly the same rules or, at least, is not exposing the club as a whole to unreasonable risks.

Second, the specific implications of **greatly expanded international capital** flows. Over the past 15 years, the outstanding stock of cross-border bank lending, as recorded in the statistics compiled by the Bank for International Settlements (BIS), has risen from under $1 trillion to $6½ trillion, that is by a factor of about seven. There has probably been even faster growth in other kinds of cross-border financial claims. This compares with an increase in nominal world GDP by a factor of about two and a half and in nominal world trade by a factor of about three. The extent of these financial exposures means that the transmission of shocks is likely to be quicker, and quite likely more damaging, than would arise purely from trade effects.

Third, the *increased emphasis on private markets*. Not only has the value of capital flows risen but the sources of funding for some developing countries and many emerging markets have shifted decisively from public to private. Correspondingly, there has been greater focus on factors contributing to the efficient functioning of private markets, including especially the availability of accurate and timely information.

Fourth, *recent experience*. The concern about knock-on effects is not simply theoretical – over the past 20 years there have been several examples of problems affecting sizeable economies which have threatened wider systemic damage. From Mexico in 1982 through the other Latin American debt crises of the 1980s, to Mexico again in 1994 and 1995, and then the East Asian debt problems of 1997 and 1998, to Russia in 1998 and Brazil in 1999 – all have called for intervention by the international financial institutions and/or by national authorities in order to contain the potential contagion.

No-one believes that formulating standards and codes, and monitoring and promoting compliance with them, is a complete response to these problems. There were clearly many contributory factors. But in most of the countries concerned there were areas where policy fell short of recognised good practice, or where features of the financial infrastructure – for example the regulatory regime – left the financial system excessively vulnerable or where there was simply not enough reliable information available for lenders and borrowers to make a proper assessment of risk. The position certainly differed from country to country. But there was sufficient commonality of experience to allow some general lessons to be drawn – and the current work on standards and codes is partly aimed at capturing those lessons.

What?

In referring to standards and codes it is worth emphasising that these are not legally enforceable rules. Most obviously this is because very little international legal machinery would be available to enforce such rules. But, even if the machinery were available, a legalistic approach might not be desirable for all sorts of reasons. (It is just worth noting, however, that in the admittedly special context of the EU, there are now many examples of transnational legally-enforceable standards and codes, including many relating to economic and financial issues.) This, of course, leaves open the question of what happens when a country fails to meet a relevant standard.

Codes have been drawn up and standards established by all sorts of bodies. This paper will not enumerate those currently recognised in the so-called Compendium. Depending on exactly what is counted, there are around 55 going on 65 in total. They can be classified in a number of different ways. In terms of subject, there are three main areas: macro-economic fundamentals; institutional and market infrastructure; and financial regulation and supervision. A list is shown in Table 1. But the list can also be divided up in other ways: between standards which are sectoral in scope (for example standards relating to banking supervision) and those which are functional (such as standards relating to corporate governance or accounting); between standards which take the form of broad principles (for example the Basle Committee's Core Principles for Effective Banking Supervision), those which spell out in more detail the intended practical application of the principles (such as the Basle Committee's Sound Practices for Loan Accounting) and those which set out detailed methodologies (such as the IMF's Special Data Dissemination Standard); and finally, the standards can be separated depending on their degree of formal international endorsement.

Table 1. International Standards

Macroeconomic Policy and Data Transparency

Code of Good Practices on Fiscal Transparency	IMF
General Data Dissemination System (GDDS)	IMF
Special Data Dissemination Standard (SDDS)	IMF
Code of Good Practices on Transparency in Monetary and Financial Policies	IMF

Institutional and Market Infrastructure

Principles of Corporate Governance	OECD
International Accounting Standards	IASC
International Standards on Auditing	IFAC
Core Principles for Systemically Important Payment Systems	CPSS
Real Time Gross Settlement Systems	CPSS
Settlement Risk in Foreign Exchange Transactions	CPSS
Report of the Committee on Interbank Netting Schemes of the Central Banks of the Group of Ten Countries (The 'Lamfalussy Report'	CPSS
OTC Derivatives: Settlement Procedures and Counterparty Risk Management	CPSS
Clearing Arrangements for Exchange-Traded Derivatives	CPSS
Delivery Versus Payment in Securities Settlement Systems	CPSS
Ten Key Principles for the Improvement of International Co-operation Regarding Financial Crimes and Regulatory Abuse	G-7
The Forty Recommendations of the Financial Action Task Force on Money Laundering	FATF

How Should We Design Deep and Liquid Markets	CGFS

Financial Regulation and Supervision

Core Principles Methodology	BCBS
Sound Practices for Banks' Interactions with Highly Leveraged Institutions	BCBS
Core Principles for Effective Banking Supervision	BCBS
International Convergence of Capital Measurement and Capital Standards	BCBS
Amendment to the Capital Accord to Incorporate Market Risks	BCBS
Supervisory Framework for the use of 'Backtesting' in Conjunction with the Internal Models Approach to Market Risk Capital Requirements	BCBS
The Supervision of Cross-Border Banking	BCBS
Minimum Standards for the Supervision of International Banking Groups and their Cross-border Establishments	BCBS
Principles for the Supervision of Banks' Foreign Establishments (the Concordat)	BCBS
Recommendations for Public Disclosure of Trading and Derivatives Activities of Banks and Securities Firms	BCBS
Sound Practices for Loan Accounting, Credit Risk Disclosure and Related Matters	BCBS
Enhancing Bank Transparency	BCBS
Principles for the Management of Credit Risk	BCBS
Framework for Internal Control Systems in Banking Organisations	BCBS
Operational Risk Management	BCBS
Risk Management for Electronic Banking and Electronic Money Activities	BCBS
Principles on the Management of Interest Rate Risk	BCBS
Risk Management Guidelines for Derivatives	BCBS
Objectives and Principles of Securities Regulation	IOSCO
IOSCO Resolution: Principles for Record Keeping, Collection of Information, Enforcement of Powers and Mutual Cooperation to Improve the Enforcement of Securities and Futures Laws	IOSCO
Methodologies for Determining Minimum Capital Standards for Internationally Active Securities Firms which Permit the Use of Models under Prescribed Conditions	IOSCO
Guidance on Information Sharing	IOSCO
Report on Co-operation Between Market Authorities and Default Procedures	IOSCO
Principles of Memoranda of Understanding	IOSCO
Recommendations for Public Disclosure of Trading and Derivatives Activities of Banks and Securities Firms	IOSCO
International Disclosure Standards for Cross-border Offerings and Initial Listings by Foreign Issuers	IOSCO
Risk Management and Control Guidance for Securities Firms and their Supervisors	IOSCO
Client Asset Protection	IOSCO
Operational and Financial Risk Management Control Mechanisms for Over-the-counter Derivatives Activities of Regulated Securities Firms	IOSCO
Securities Activity on the Internet	IOSCO)
The Application of the Tokyo Communiqué to Exchange-Traded Financial Derivatives Contracts	IOSCO

Principles for the Supervision of Operators of Collective Investment Schemes	IOSCO
Report on Investment Management Principles for the Regulation of Collective Investment Schemes and Explanatory Memorandum	IOSCO
Co-ordination between Cash and Derivative Markets: Contract Design of Derivative Products on Stock Indices and Measures to Mini	IOSCO
Insurance Core Principles	IAIS
Principles on the Supervision of Insurance Activities on the Internet	IAIS
Supervisory Standard on Group Co-ordination	IAIS
Insurance Core Principles Methodology	IAIS
Principles for the Conduct of Insurance Business	IAIS
Supervisory Standard on On-Site Inspections	IAIS
Supervisory Standard on Licensing	IAIS
Guidance on Insurance Regulation and Supervision for Emerging Market Economies	IAIS
Model Memorandum of Understanding	IAIS
Principles Applicable to the Supervision of International Insurers and Insurance Groups and their Cross-Border Operations	IAIS
Supervisory Standard on Asset Management by Insurance Companies	IAIS
Supervisory Standard on Derivatives	IAIS
Supervision of Financial Conglomerates	JF
Intra-Group Transactions and Exposure Principles	JF
Risk Concentration Principles	JF

All this illustrates the diversity of approach reflected under the general heading of standards and codes. The length of the list also indicates that it would be a tall order indeed to try to make progress on implementation uniformly across the entire list.

How?

The infeasibility of an 'across-the-board' approach for 50 or so standards over 180 countries is of course well recognised, and there are several ways of making the task more manageable. The first has been to identify a much smaller group of 12 key standards. A second has been to acknowledge that different standards have different priorities for different countries, and that these priorities are likely to change over time. Indeed, in some cases there is probably a rather strict sequencing implicit in the standards themselves – it would, for example, be foolish to put a lot of effort into the more esoteric aspects of prudential banking supervision in the absence of a proper accounting framework for the measurement of asset values, capital and so on. The 'key' standards are key in the sense that the aim of meeting them would make sense for many, even if not all, countries.

The second point to make under the heading of 'How?' is that, without someone to orchestrate and monitor the process of implementation, there is a risk that momentum will be lost. Even if everyone accepted in principle that all the standards and codes were sensible – and that would probably be an optimistic assumption – there are many potential difficulties in turning theory into practice, sufficient certainly to threaten that the process of implementation would run into the sands. Who should this orchestrator be? No institution has an operational remit which runs across all the areas covered by the various standards and codes. But the IMF probably comes closest – *pace* those who would curb its role – and it is arguable that the IMF is the appropriate body to take on the task. The task, however, is to monitor and co-ordinate the overall process, not to be responsible for each of the individual parts. As Jack Boorman of the Fund aptly describes it, the IMF would maintain the 'loose-leaf binder' into which reviews and assessments of progress, produced in some cases by the IMF but in many cases by others, could be slotted. The so-called ROSC process, and the work on FSAPs, involving both the IMF and the World Bank, are practical manifestations of this approach.

A third important, but contentious, aspect of implementation is the question of incentives. Why should a country commit itself to observe these standards and codes? The general incentive, if the standards and codes are well formulated, should be that compliance will improve national economic performance. But there is an issue whether, beyond that, there are specific incentives which the private sector or the public sector might provide. This paper will not enter into the detail of the arguments, except to note that one approach to the question is from the point of view of the identification, measurement and management of risk. It would be quite reasonable for private lenders and investors to take into account compliance with relevant standards and codes if they thought that it affected the risks they were running. It would also seem reasonable, on the same basis, that public sector lenders should take these considerations into account. But public sector lenders also need to have in mind 'systemic' externalities, that is, that the failure of a country to meet its obligations may threaten the financial system generally and require their intervention to contain the consequential systemic damage. To that extent, they may put more weight than the private sector on compliance with standards and codes as providing some protection against this risk.

A final, and again important, consideration under the heading of 'How?' is that of technical assistance and training. Whatever the incentives, there are bound to be limits for many countries to their technical capacity to implement standards and codes; and there may also be constraints on the capacity of the IFIs and/or standard setters to monitor implementation. In turning the standards and codes programme into reality, it will be necessary to address these resource issues.

Conclusions

This paper has been pitched at a rather general level but it is intended to give a flavour of some of the issues which have arisen in discussions about the formulation and implementation of standards and codes. Overall, the setting out of these standards, and transparency about their implementation, could make a significant contribution to strengthening the international financial system.

Three further points are relevant to any discussion of standards and codes in the global financial system.

◆ First, better information about borrowers is only half the story. The counterpart is the need for lenders and investors to make proper use of that information. The evidence on the extent to which they do this is patchy but it certainly cannot be taken for granted that all lenders, even all major lenders, will give due weight to additional information when it is available. There is an important challenge to find incentives which can be applied to lenders so as to encourage them to pursue improved risk-management practices in this area.

◆ Second, effective implementation of the standards and codes programme involves many different parties. The official interest is reflected in various international committees; but it is important also that the private sector should be engaged. For that reason, a number of initiatives under the general heading of 'outreach' are underway, aimed at telling private market participants what is going on, seeking their views on what information and in what form they would find most useful, and encouraging them to make use of it. The IMF and the Financial Stability Forum have been particularly active in promoting such dialogue.

◆ Third, it is important to have a realistic timetable for carrying through the standards and codes programme as it has now been set out. It is not something which can be delivered overnight, within a few months or even within a year or two. It is bound to be a long-term exercise. Recognising that, however, should not become a reason for delaying progress now.

The Disturbing Interaction between the Madness of Crowds and the Risk Management of Banks

Avinash Persaud

Summary

In the international financial arena, G-7 policy-makers chant three things: more market-sensitive risk management, stronger prudential standards and improved transparency. The message is that we do not need a new world order, but we can improve the workings of the existing one. While many believe this is an inadequate response to the financial crises of the last two decades, few argue against risk management, prudence and transparency. Perhaps more should. The underlying idea behind this holy trinity is that it better equips markets to reward good behaviour and penalise bad across governments and market players. However, while the market is discerning in the long run, there is now compelling evidence that in the short run markets find it hard to distinguish between the good and the unsustainable, market participants herd and contagion is common. Critically, in a herding environment, tighter market-sensitive risk-management systems and more transparency actually make markets less stable and more prone to crisis. This perverse response may help to explain the growing instability of the financial system. The system has been in crisis in almost four of the last ten years. Demands for the daily release of foreign exchange reserves should be tempered, and policy-makers and regulators should support investors who do not herd – foreign direct investors, equity portfolio investors and, surprisingly, hedge funds.

A Cyclical Debate

The debate on the reform of the international financial system follows a cycle. In the middle of each crisis – and there have been at least six since the debt crisis which started in Mexico in 1982 – there are deafening demands for the wholesale reform of the entire international financial system. A few months on from the end of each crisis these demands fade. There were clear parallels between calls made in previous crises and those made in the thick of the last crisis for the IMF to become a lender of last resort, injecting substantial liquidity in times of crisis, and for hedge funds to be regulated. Every crisis inspires plans for a new financial architecture and, as the crisis ends, most of these plans are tidied away.

Table 1. Global financial crises in the 1990s

Date	Crisis	Countries where the real exchange rate fell by more than 10 per cent over one month
1992–93	'EMS'	UK, Italy, Spain, Portugal, Sweden, Finland, Denmark, Norway, Belgium, France, Ireland, India, Venezuela
1994–95	'Tequila'	Colombia, Venezuela, Mexico, Turkey, Japan
1997–99	'Asia'	Thailand, Philippines, Indonesia, Malaysia, Taiwan, Korea, Brazil Colombia, Israel, Peru, South Africa, Zimbabwe, Russia, Sweden, Switzerland, Spain

Underlying this cycle of debate is that while the demand to make systemic changes is naturally strong in the middle of a crisis, the consensus on what is wrong and what to do is generally weak. Moreover, while recent crises have appeared sharper and more global than before, they have been more short-lived. Before a consensus on what to do to avoid crises can grow, they are over, and countries previously in crisis begin to enjoy economic rebound and the return of international capital flows. This was not the case during the Latin American debt crisis of the mid-1980s or after the EMS crisis in 1992–93 when economic recovery was held back by self-imposed fiscal restraint and a cheap dollar. But it was the case in the last two crises in Mexico and Asia (see Chart 1). We also live in an age where ambitions are limited. We no longer walk on the moon. In this environment, the view that often gains ground a few months after the crisis is that there are risks in meddling with a financial system that works most of the time, and that there are things that can be safely done to improve the workings of the market the rest of the time.

The proposals that emerge post-crisis, therefore, tend to focus on making it easier for the market to reward good behaviour and penalise bad behaviour. The emphasis is not on changing the rules of the game, but on strengthening the players: stronger risk management, more prudential standards and improved transparency. One of the key responses of the Interim Committee of the IMF to the latest crisis and the desire to avoid another one was the adoption on 26 September 1999 of a new Code of Good Practices on Transparency in Monetary and Financial Policies. Incidentally, these measures are all relatively inexpensive to implement. There is declining political support for large packages of tax-payers money to bail out foreign countries in trouble.

Chart 1. The rapid rebound in Asian GDP

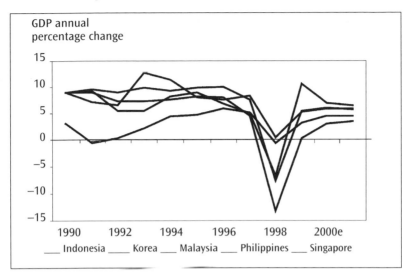

How More Market-sensitive Risk Management Can Create Risk

While many believe that risk management, prudential standards and transparency are probably not enough to avoid future crises, they believe these measures will probably help to provide the right discipline for governments and can surely do no harm. These measures are likely to be a positive force in the long run when markets are good at discerning between the good and bad. But in the short run, there is growing evidence that market participants find it hard to distinguish between the good and the unsustainable, that they often herd and that contagion from one crisis to another is common. The problem is that in a world of 'herding', tighter market-sensitive risk-management regulations and improved transparency can, perversely, turn events from bad to worse, aggravating and perhaps even initiating a crisis. How can this happen?

Let us explore the interaction between herding, risk management and transparency in bank lending. It is important to note that while there are strong parallels between the behaviour of herding bankers and herding investors in general, bank lending remains a powerful feature of modern-day crises. For example, the five Asian crisis countries – Thailand, Malaysia, South Korea, Indonesia and the Philippines – received $47.8 billion in foreign bank loans in 1996. In 1997, banks withdrew $29.9 billion – a net turnaround of almost $80 billion in one year. In contrast, portfolio flows remained positive throughout 1997.

The growing fashion in risk management, supported by the Basle Committee on Banking Supervision, is a move away from discretionary judgements about risk and a move to more quantitative and market-sensitive approaches. (See *The Supervisory Treatment of Market Risks*, Basle Committee on Banking Supervision, 1993.) This is well illustrated by how banks now tend to manage market risks by setting a DEAR limit – daily earnings at risk. DEAR answers the question: 'How much can I lose with, say, a 1 per cent probability over the next day'. It is calculated by taking the bank's portfolio of positions and estimating the future distribution of daily returns based on past measures of market correlation and volatility. Both rising volatility and rising correlation will increase the potential loss of the portfolio, increasing DEAR. Falling volatility and correlation will do the opposite. Banks set a DEAR limit – the maximum dollar amount they are prepared to put at risk of losing with a 1 per cent probability. When DEAR exceeds the limit, the bank reduces exposure, often by switching into less volatile and less correlated assets. (See *RiskMetrics Technical Manual*, RiskMetrics Group, London, 1999.)

Figure 1. Representation of VAR: histogram of portfolio values

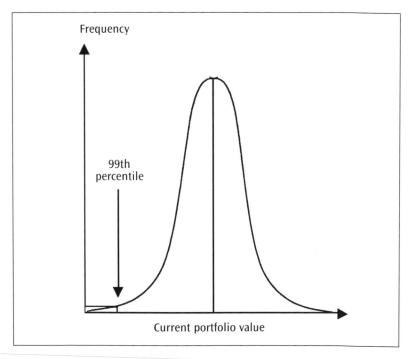

Herding behaviour means that banks or investors like to buy what others are buying, sell what others are selling and own what others own. There are three main explanations for why bankers and investors herd. Firstly, in a world of uncertainty, the best way of exploiting the information of others is by copying what they are doing. Secondly, bankers and investors are often measured and rewarded by relative performance so it literally does not pay a risk-averse player to stray too far from the pack. Thirdly, investors and bankers are more likely to be sacked for being wrong and alone than being wrong and in company. (For further explanations of herding see *Investor Behaviour in the October 1987 Stock Market Crash: Survey Evidence* by R. Shiller, NBER discussion paper 2446, 1990.)

Figure 2. A vicious cycle of herding and DEAR limits

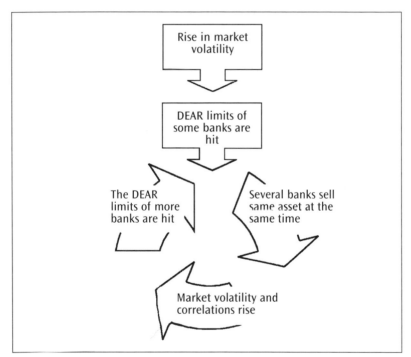

Imagine that over time a herd of banks have acquired both Korean property and UK technology stocks. Imagine too that some bad news causes volatility in UK technology stocks and the banks most heavily invested there find that their DEAR limits are hit. As these banks try and reduce their DEAR by selling the same stocks at the same time, there are dramatic declines in prices and rises in volatility in both markets and in the correlation between Korean and UK markets. Rising volatility and correlation triggers the DEAR limits of banks less heavily invested in these markets. As they join the selling milieu, prices, volatility and correlation move further in a self-feeding cycle.

The key to this environment is that market participants behave strategically in relation to one another, but DEAR measures risk 'statically', without strategic considerations. Previous volatility and correlations were measured over a period of time when the herd gradually built up and are therefore almost certain to underestimate the impact on prices, volatility and correlations when many investors sell the same asset at the same time. This strategic behaviour can be modelled more formally using game theory. (Some attempts to do so can be found in 'Risk management with interdependent choice' by Stephen Morris and Hyun Song Shin, *Oxford Review of Economic Policy*, Autumn 1999.)

Let us add another strategic dimension to this spiralling nightmare. Further assume that the country has recently signed up to the Special Data Dissemination Standard (SDDS) – one of the lasting responses of the 1995 Tequila crisis – and the 1999 Code of Good Practice and, as a result, has started publishing its foreign exchange reserves daily. In this case bankers and investors with more modest exposures would observe that as risks grow – prices are falling and volatility rising – other bankers and investors are leaving the country rapidly. In this heightened environment they will view the country's loss of reserves as doubly increasing the risk that they will be left wrong and alone. This will trigger a further rush for the exit.

The reason why this is a major challenge to the current regulatory framework is that herding is frequent and that even short-lived financial crises have real economic impact. While herding behaviour is hard to prove directly, given the paucity of reliable data on the positions of financial institutions, there is a now a growing body of evidence that markets behave as if market participants herd.

In the foreign exchange markets, for example, if we define a crash as a 10 per cent fall in the real exchange rate over three months, there have been 78 crashes across 72 countries since the EMS crisis began in September 1992. These are not distributed evenly over time, or distributed with deteriorating fundamentals, but they cluster. Contagion is rife with 70 per cent of crashes occurring in just three years. This contagion does not move predictably along the lines of trade, but along the lines of shared investors. The stepping stones of the most recent crisis, for example, were from Thailand and Indonesia to Korea, on to Russia and then to Brazil. These countries share very little trade. Furthermore, crashes are invariably preceded by booms as the herd moves into place. Chart 2 shows the number of foreign exchange crashes per year across 72 countries as bars and the annual cross-border portfolio flows into emerging markets as a line. Note how investors rushed into emerging markets in 1995 and 1996, prior to the crashes in 1997 and 1998.

Chart 2. 'Crashes' and 'booms' in the foreign exchange market

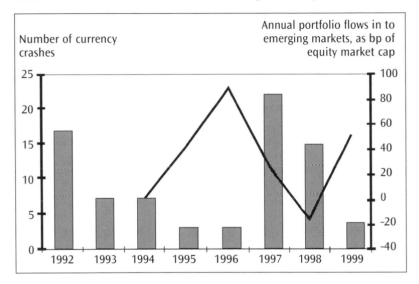

Further evidence of herding and the problems of a static value-at-risk analysis can be found by looking at the distribution of daily market returns. In Chart 3, we imagine we are a risk manager in January 1997 looking at the distribution of daily returns of a portfolio of OECD currencies versus the dollar over the previous five years. The distribution is well behaved and fairly symmetrical – though not around zero. According to this actual distribution she would expect a more than 1 per cent decline in this portfolio's value in a day around 5 per cent of the time. Three years later and if she survived, she would have found that her portfolio fell by more than 1 per cent in a day more than 10 per cent of the time and the distribution would look very different – as shown in Chart 4. (It can be shown that the difference between these two distributions follows a beta distribution consistent with herding behaviour.)

The predominance of herding behaviour and its lethal combination with the practice of DEAR limits may explain why the 1990s have been such a decade of financial dislocation: the financial system has been in crisis for 40 out of the 120 months, or 33 per cent of the time. This instability has real economic impact. Although international portfolio flows have

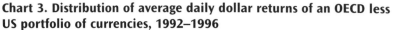

Chart 3. Distribution of average daily dollar returns of an OECD less US portfolio of currencies, 1992–1996

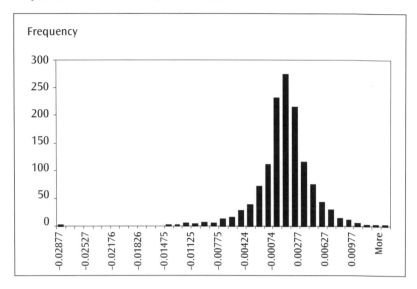

Chart 4. Distribution of average daily dollar returns of an OECD less US portfolio of currencies, 1997–1999

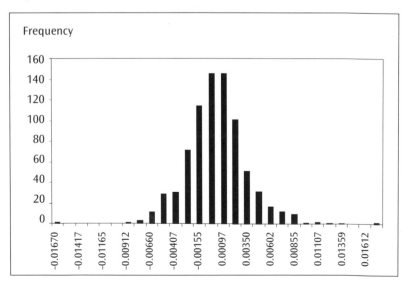

recovered from dips in 1998, they remain highly concentrated in just five markets: Hong Kong, Korea, Singapore and Taiwan – hardly the most capital-needy countries given either their high domestic savings and big current account surpluses. Many other markets have found it hard to raise foreign capital.

These financial crises also have a direct impact on GDP. For example, while there has been a strong rebound in GDP in 1999 in Asia in general, and in South Korea in particular, the rebound has not offset the loss of GDP during the crisis period. One way of estimating the lost GDP of the Asian crisis is to estimate where GDP would be today if Asian economies had continued the more modest but sustainable growth rates experienced in the five years before their current account deficits began to widen in 1993–94. Were it not for the crisis and its preceding boom, GDP would be an aggregate of $130 billion higher in South Korea, Thailand, Malaysia and Indonesia. Another measure of this lasting impact is the elevation of poverty levels in Asia today compared with 1997.

The paradox is that if one or two banks followed a DEAR limit and others did not, those banks would have an effective risk-management system that at the margin would support the financial system. But if every bank follows the same approach, given that these banks follow each other into and out of markets, the DEAR limit will contribute to systemic risk. It is ironic, therefore, that the Basle Committee on Banking Supervision is supporting the rapid adoption of these systems across all banks. (See 'An internal model-based approach to market risk capital requirements', Bank for International Settlements, Basle, 1995.) There is a further paradox with transparency. The more herding investors and banks know about what each other are up to, the more unstable markets may become. In the long run, transparency and DEAR limits are a good development, but they are harmful in the short run in the context of herding behaviour.

What Should Policy-Makers and Regulators Do?

Herding presents a classic example of the need for intervention. The individual incentives of herding investors create systemic risks. Moreover, if regulators were so co-ordinated that they behaved like one global regulator, they would be best placed to make an intervention. Through the privileged formation they have as a regulator of individual bank balance sheets they know when banks are herding. This does require a different focus. Today regulators are warned about whether banks in their jurisdiction have exposures that threaten themselves, not whether banks around the world have the same exposure, which threatens a foreign market that could become contagious. If this information were made public, in the context of herding investors, random shocks could quickly evolve into financial crises. But how should regulators respond if they notice herding in a particular market? They should require the bank to put aside an extra amount of capital for 'strategic risk' without specifying which markets carry that risk. Applying tighter risk-management requirements for those specific markets in which the herd has appeared will only make the stampede more vicious when negative news strikes.

It is arguable that regulators have actually promoted herding through risk-management systems. They may also have done so in their zeal for disclosure of bank positions and central bank reserves. Indeed, there is a role for one unregulated investor who is encouraged to buy near the bottom of markets through the absence of risk, capital disclosure and credit concerns. Such investors would make the system safer but would be high risk and so should be restricted to those who can afford to lose. If this investor had to be invented she would look something like a hedge fund. Interestingly, as the big-betting hedge funds have been undermined by the disclosure and credit policies of banks, market liquidity has fallen and volatility has risen. Just as the big macro hedge funds fade away we may find that they supported the market as much as they exploited it.

Those who are unable to stomach regulators promoting hedge funds will be relieved to note that there are other kinds of flows that do not herd so much – foreign direct investment, for example. Further, during the Mexican and Asian crises, equity portfolio flows also revealed less herding than bond flows. It would appear that bond investors are keen to get out before they are held in by a debt moratorium or orderly work-out. This raises some interesting questions for those trying to build in burden-sharing and orderly work-out provisions into bond constitutions.

Transparency in data and governance is clearly a good thing in the long run and promotes correct behaviour by governments. Governments should be encouraged to disclose more information every month and quarter, but not on a daily basis. In an environment of herding investors, there is not a good case for insisting that countries release central bank reserve data with such high frequency. It is telling that during the EMS crisis, many of the developed countries who had just adopted the Code of Good Practice on Transparency found it helpful to delay the monthly publication of their official reserves or to camouflage their information. Small vulnerable emerging markets will find it even more helpful not to publish their reserves every day.

International Transparency and Regulatory Challenges

Stephany Griffith-Jones and Amar Bhattacharya

Much of the focus of activity since the Asian and other crises has been on measures to decrease vulnerability at the national level in recipient countries. (For an excellent analysis, see the *Working Group Report on Capital Flows*, Financial Stability Forum, 2000.)

However, it seems equally important to diminish vulnerability at the international level, as in recent crises imperfections in international capital markets played at least as large a role (if not a larger one) as mistakes and weaknesses in recipient economies. In this sense, it is disappointing that action at the international level, particularly in implementation of better transparency regulation, has till now been far less and slower than actions in recipient economies. A very positive step has, however, been taken with the creation of the Financial Stability Forum; it is, however, very problematic that developing countries have no participation in its meetings or decisions, even though they are invited to participate in its working groups. Representation of developing countries in the FSF would be highly desirable both for reasons of legitimacy and because it would provide the body with a wider range of expertise and perspectives.

At the international level, there are two challenges: (a) improving transparency of markets by providing relevant information on a timely basis, an effort that would be symmetrical to the large effort being undertaken on improving transparency in country economies; and (b) improving regulation of markets, where current regulations are imperfect or where gaps exist.

Better Transparency

As regards improved transparency on markets, a number of important actions have been taken. These include a meeting between compilers and users of data, held at the IMF in February 2000, to discuss data issues on capital flows.

Areas where improved information is urgent include highly leveraged institutions (HLIs) and over-the-counter derivatives (OTCS) as these are particularly opaque. But it is also essential to make progress on more complete and timely information on exposures by other institutional investors and banks to developing countries, as this is essential for better policy-making in general, and particularly so in times of crises.

As regards HLIs, the Report of the FSF Working Group on HLIs issued valuable recommendations on disclosure. These focus mainly on public exposure (also recommended by other reports, including a report by the International Organisation of Securities Commissions (IOSCO) Technical Committee). Two proposals are currently before the US Congress which seek to impose disclosure requirements only on large funds, which could have systemic importance, without disclosure of proprietary information. These efforts have been endorsed by the FSF working party, which also calls on all jurisdictions to consider the adequacy of their disclosure requirements and introduce, where necessary, appropriate changes to ensure that major hedge funds are subject to complementary disclosure requirements; this recommendation also applies to offshore centres, particularly those which currently host large unregulated hedge funds.

Because the build-up of leverage was not confined to hedge funds, the working group on HLIs has rightly stressed the need to enhance disclosure of risk exposures by all participants in financial markets, both regulated and unregulated; these include banks, insurance companies, securities firms, mutual funds and hedge funds. A voluntary study is being organised in this crucial field, with a final report to be prepared by the end of 2000, on appropriate steps to be taken to improve the state of disclosures by all intermediaries. The measures may require changes in regulatory practices or in the law. This seems an extremely valuable step, which hopefully will be implemented quickly.

Better Regulation
The case for additional regulation

There is growing support for the view that the process of international financial intermediation has a second-best element, in which welfare for both source and recipient countries can be increased by regulatory changes (through measures in source and/or recipient countries), which would reduce excessive lending or investing. It is noteworthy that the Chairman of the US Federal Reserve Board, Alan Greenspan, proposed, for the case of interbank lending, that it could be appropriate for either borrowing countries or lending ones to impose reserve requirements to 'deter aberrant borrowing: sovereigns could charge an explicit premium, or could impose reserve requirements, earning low or even zero interest rates, on interbank liabilities. Increasing the capital charge on lending banks, instead of on borrowing banks, might also be effective."[1]

There is growing recognition that it may often be desirable to regulate excessive surges of potentially reversible capital flows in recipient countries. Indeed, an important part of the responsibility for discouraging excessive reversible inflows – as well as managing them – lies with the recipient countries. However, the experience of the 1990s, with a very large scale of international funds, compared to the small size of developing country markets, leads to the question whether measures to discourage excessive short-term flows by recipient countries are sufficient to deal with capital surges and the risk of their reversal.

Aizenman and Turnovsky (1999) have formalised such analysis by developing a rigorous model that analyses the impact via externalities of reserve requirements on international loans (both in lending and recipient countries) on the welfare of both categories of countries. They thus evaluate the macro-economic impact of reserve requirements in a second-best world, where there is moral hazard due to likely bail-outs on the lender's side and sovereign risk on the borrower's side; both generate large negative externalities on welfare. The general conclusion of their model is that the introduction of a reserve requirement in either the source or recipient country reduces the risk of default and raises welfare in both countries.

Regulatory changes can help smooth capital flows to emerging markets, without discouraging them excessively. This is in contrast to views based on a belief that crises in emerging markets are due only to moral hazard, and that the appropriate way to combat such moral hazard is by scaling down the role of the IMF in providing financial packages before and during crises. However, such a reduction of the role of the IMF could either make crises even more costly and/or lead to a sharp reduction in private flows to developing countries. These are both highly undesirable effects which could significantly diminish welfare, particularly, but not only, in the developing economies, as well as undermine support for open economies and market-based economic policies in developing economies. Therefore, an approach based on better regulation is clearly better and more welfare enhancing than one which cuts back the role of the IMF.

---

[1] Remarks by Alan Greenspan before the 34th Annual Conference of the Federal Reserve Bank of Chicago, 7 May 1998.

Filling gaps

The broad welfare case for applying reserve requirements in both source and recipient countries can also be applied to institutional investors and, in particular, to mutual funds, which became increasingly important in relation to banks in the 1990s. This growing importance occurred both within the developed countries, and particularly within the USA, where mutual funds receive more than 50 per cent of total deposits in the financial system, and in capital flows from developed to developing countries (see d'Arista and Griffith-Jones, 2000).

The narrowing of differences between banks and institutional investors like mutual funds, and the fact that securities markets and thus mutual funds also have access to the lender of last resort – nationally in the USA but more importantly in our context also internationally, due to the frequent rescue packages put together by the IMF in recent serious currency crises – suggest the importance of improving prudential standards for institutional investors such as mutual funds.

As regards portfolio flows to emerging markets, there is an important regulatory gap, as at present there is no international regulatory framework which takes account of market or credit risks on flows originating in institutional investors, such as mutual funds (and more broadly for flows originating in non-bank institutions). This important gap needs to be filled, both to protect retail investors in developed countries and to protect developing countries from the negative effects of excessively large and potentially reversible portfolio flows.

Institutional investors like mutual funds, given the very liquid nature of their investments, can play an important role in contributing to developing country currency crises. (For recent evidence, see Kaminsky, Schmukler and Lyon, 2000.) It seems important, therefore, to introduce some regulation to discourage excessive surges of portfolio flows. This could perhaps best be achieved by a variable risk-weighted cash requirement for institutional investors, such as mutual funds. These cash requirements would be placed as interest-bearing deposits in commercial banks. Introducing a dynamic risk-weighted cash requirement for mutual funds (and perhaps for other institutional investors) is in the mainstream of current regulatory thinking and would require that standards be provided by relevant regulatory authorities and/or agreed internationally. The guidelines for macro-economic risk, which would determine the cash requirement, would take into account vulnerability variables as defined by the IMF and the BIS.

The fact that the level of required cash reserves would vary with the level of countries' perceived 'macro-economic risk' would make it relatively more profitable to invest more in countries with good fundamentals and relatively less profitable to invest in countries with more problematic macro or financial sector fundamentals. If these fundamentals in a country deteriorated, investment would decline gradually, which hopefully would force an early correction of policy and a resumption of flows. Though the requirement for cash reserves on mutual funds' assets invested in emerging markets could increase the cost of raising foreign capital for them, this would be compensated for by their having a more stable supply of funds, at a more stable cost. Furthermore, this counter-cyclical smoothing of flows would hopefully discourage massive and sudden reversals.

The September 1998 Emerging Markets IOSCO Report on Causes, Effects and Regulatory Implications of Financial and Economic Turbulence in Emerging Markets has in fact described in some detail and evaluated rather positively the above proposal. This report emphasised that 'there appears to be scope – and an urgent need for further work. This is very likely to require a multilateral effort – i.e. by regulators from both source and recipient countries in collaboration with the industry.'

As regards HLIs, the FSF working group on HLIs rightly focused on two problems: systemic risk linked to high leverage and reduction of the market, and the economic impact of the collapse of unregulated HLIs. Particular emphasis was placed on HLI activities in small and medium-sized open economies where the potential damage that can be caused by large and concentrated positions can seriously amplify market pressures.

The FSF working group considered formal direct regulation of currently unregulated institutions. This would include a licensing system, minimum capital and liquidity standards, large exposure limits, minimum standards for risk management and even an enforcement regime with fines for transgressions.

Such regulation was seen to have several very desirable effects (such as regular oversight over HLIs and a reduction in the likelihood of disruptive market events) but, due to what were seen as both philosophical and practical problems, the working group did not recommend applying a system of direct regulation to currently unregulated HLIS at this stage, although it did not reject the possibility of establishing such a regime in the future. It emphasised that the failure to carry through its recommendations would prompt such reconsideration.

The philosophical objection relates to the fact that direct regulation would not be aimed at investor protection (as investors are sufficiently wealthy or sophisticated to do their own due diligence), but on the mitigation of systemic risk. However, it could be argued that mitigation of systemic risk is also an increasingly valid regulatory aim. There are also practical objections, including how to avoid leakage through offshore centres. However, current efforts to improve and complete regulation in offshore centres should help overcome those problems. (See discussion in the FSF Working Group Report on Offshore Centres.) Other practical issues are more technical and more valid, including the need to adapt capital adequacy and large exposure rules to the specific risk profile of HLIs. This should be done in such a way that any regulatory capital requirement does not adversely affect the efficiency and liquidity of markets in which HLIs are significant participants. This seems particularly important in a context in which several large hedge funds have been wound down, which may diminish some of the negative impacts they had in recent crises, but it could, according to some observers, deprive markets of contrarian actors, who have useful roles to play in stopping the deepening crises.

The need to regulate HLIs directly must be revisited, partly in relation to the implementation (or not) of other measures recommended by the working group and their perceived impact. These measure include:

◆ stronger counter-party risk management;

◆ stronger hedge fund risk management;

◆ enhanced regulatory oversight of HLI credit providers;

◆ greater risk sensitivity in bank capital adequacy;

◆ building a firmer market infrastructure;

◆ better public disclosure of HLIs (discussed above);

◆ enhanced national surveillance of financial market activity at the national level to identify rising leverage and concerns relating to market dynamic;

◆ taking appropriate preventive measures, where necessary, and putting in place good practice guidelines for foreign exchange trading, which could be adapted in individual emerging markets.

Removing regulatory distortions and dampening exuberance of bank lending

As regards bank lending, there has firstly been concern that the 1988 Basle Capital Accord contributed to the build-up of short-term bank lending and its reversal in East Asia and elsewhere, due to significantly lower capital adequacy requirements for short-term lending than for long-term lending. The new proposal, published in June 1999, attempts to address this distortion by reducing somewhat (though perhaps not sufficiently) the differential between capital adequacy for short-term and other lending. However, the new Basle recommendations, though including many positive elements (see, for example, Caillous and Griffith-Jones, 1999), also contain suggestions that have been widely seen as problematic. These include increasing the role of rating agencies to determine country weightings for capital adequacy, which could aggravate the pro-cyclical nature of bank lending and thus encourage larger surges and larger reversals. This is clearly an undesirable outcome.

There is important evidence that rating agencies act in a volatile and, especially, pro-cyclical fashion. If that were the case, reliance on ratings in the new system would exacerbate boom-bust cycles and could undermine the stability of the financial system.

The most recent evidence of this pro-cyclical pattern is the Asian crisis. Indeed, as pointed by various authors (see, for example, Turner, 2000; Cornford, 2000; Reisen, 1999), rating agencies failed to downgrade the East Asian countries before the crisis but then worsened it because they brought down the ratings as the crisis unfolded. Reisen and von Maltzan (1999) assess the impact on the market of the publications of ratings by the main rating agencies and find that sovereign ratings lag behind, rather than lead, the market.

These problems should not, however, put in question the need to reform the 1988 Accord. The current system has fixed weightings which do not adjust with the cycle. In the event of a recession the increased amounts of bad loans (which are usually not fully covered by provisions) will impact upon the lending bank's capital and can lead to decreased lending if the bank is already facing a relatively low capital asset ratio and, as is likely in a recession, is unable to raise new capital.

Thus the answer may lie in the implementation of an explicit counter-cyclical mechanism which would, in boom periods, and in contrast to ratings, dampen excess bank lending. Counter-cyclical elements can also be introduced in regulating other actors (see above for mutual funds). On the contrary, in periods of slowdown and of scarcity of finance, the new mechanism should not further accentuate the decline in lending, as exemplified by the 1997–98 Asian crisis, but rather encourage it.

There would be two linked objectives in introducing elements of counter-cyclical regulation. One would be to help smooth capital flows; the other would be to smooth the domestic impact of volatile capital flows on the domestic financial system and, therefore, on the real economy. Introducing counter-cyclical elements into regulation would help build a link between the more micro-economic risks on which regulators have tended to focus till recently and the macro-economic risks which are becoming increasingly important, both nationally and internationally.[1] Counter-cyclical elements in regulation related to bank lending could be applied, either internationally, nationally or at both levels.

Several mechanisms could be used to introduce a counter-cyclical element into the regulation of bank lending. One mechanism would be to get the required capital ratio higher in times of boom and to allow banks to use the additional cushion provided by the higher capital ratio, so that they could sustain lending in times of recession at a lower capital asset ratio (when increased bad loans are likely to be reducing their capital). Some practical difficulties may arise in implementing such a mechanism, of which the most serious may be getting international agreement on a general formula for cyclically adjusted capital asset ratios.

A second mechanism for introducing counter-cyclical elements in bank lending regulation is for regulators to encourage higher general provision for possible loan losses (that is, provision which is subtracted from equity capital in the books of the bank) to cover normal cyclical risks (Turner, 2000). This would allow for provision built up in good times to be used in bad times, without affecting reported capital. The way to ensure this would be to maintain higher general provisioning in relation to all loans. The main problem with this, according to Turner, may be that tax laws often limit the tax deductibility of precautionary provisioning. However, it is possible to change such tax laws, as was indeed done in the late 1980s in the UK. A third mechanism, especially relevant for domestic bank lending, is for regulators to place caps on the value of assets (such as real estate or stocks and shares) acceptable as collateral, when the value of such assets has risen sharply in a boom and is at risk of declining sharply in a recession. Rules could be used such as averaging values for the last five years, or accepting only 50 per cent of current prices in the peak period of a boom. The latter mechanism seems to have the least problems of implementation (indeed, reportedly, it is already applied in some jurisdictions, for example Hong Kong).

A fourth possible counter-cyclical mechanism is that, as suggested by McKinnon and Pill, monetary authorities could monitor and try to limit or discourage lending for property, construction and personal consump-

---

[1] We thank Andrew Crockett for his suggestive remarks on this point.

tion, as these items tend to increase substantially in booms, where they often become a major factor. A possible implementation problem would be that it may be difficult to verify final use of credit, so that such measures could be partially evaded.

Furthermore, regulators should be flexible in the downturn, particularly to allow banks to easily use cushions (for example of capital or of provisioning) in times of recession; it may even be advisable, if a recession is very serious, to allow ratios to fall below normally required levels, in order to help sustain lending, on the understanding that they will be rebuilt as soon as the economy starts recovering. A tension may arise here between the regulatory concerns about individual bank liquidity and solvency, and the macro-economic externalities of their actions, particularly in recessions. Specific issues seem to require further study. How best can the distinction between a temporary boom and a permanent increase in growth be made? After what period of 'boom' should regulatory changes be introduced? How large should such changes be? What are the best mechanisms through which counter-cyclical measures can be introduced – flexible capital adequacy ratios, higher provisioning against losses or more 'realistic' pricing of collateral? Should such measures be introduced for both international and domestic lending, or preferably for one of them? This paper provides only initial thoughts on these important issues.

Crises and Global Financial Consolidation: Lessons for International Regulation?[1]

Philip Turner

Introduction

Two key elements have a bearing on the international regulatory challenges for financial systems in the emerging markets. The first element is the weakness of domestic financial institutions and infrastructure revealed in recent crises. The second element is the pressures that arise for financial systems from what, for want of a better term, can be called 'global consolidation' – the emergence of fewer and bigger banks, the concentration of securities trading in a few centres and so on. These trends are somewhat ambiguous, but nevertheless have an important bearing on some long-term policy choices in the emerging markets.

Each trend has been much discussed in recent years, but the interaction between the two has received somewhat less attention. For instance, we can draw lessons from recent crises for the supervision of local banks; but how are supervisory strategies modified by the substantial presence in the local market of large international banks? Capital market development provides another instance. We have learnt that emerging markets need to develop their local capital markets – especially their bond markets; but does the trend towards consolidation mean that many, small local capital markets will become less and less viable? This paper raises some of these questions, but provides rather few answers.

Lessons from Crises

The first and most obvious lesson of repeated crises is that capital flows are volatile. This volatility can take the form of large-scale swings in capital movements or of sizeable movements in asset prices to forestall heavy *ex ante* flows. Small open economies are particularly vulnerable to disruption by large flows of international capital. And they are likely to remain so. When the liberalisation of capital flows began to spread globally

---

[1]Views expressed in this paper do not necessarily reflect the views of the BIS. Thanks to Marc Klau for statistical work and Emma Warrack for efficient secretarial assistance.

in the 1980s, the volatility that arose surprised many observers. The response at that time was often to dismiss volatility as transitional – markets would settle down once macro-economic stability was restored and when financial institutions and governments had become more accustomed to the new world of liberal capital markets. After all, capital markets had not been free since before World War I and the situation would take some getting used to. The 1990s was indeed largely a decade in which macro-economic stability was restored – progressively almost everywhere. Yet volatility has persisted. As far as can be judged, financial asset prices have been more volatile in the last decade than in the global capital market that prevailed before World War I. For instance, bond yields even in relatively stable low-inflation countries have been much more volatile than they were pre-1913 – despite more stable inflation in the recent period (Table 1). Volatility is probably intrinsic to modern financial markets, and arises even in the markets of countries that are well-managed.

Table 1. The variability of interest rates in two periods of globalisation

	Inflation rate		Long-term interest rate		Short-term interest rate	
	Average	Standard deviation*	Average	Standard deviation*	Average	Standard deviation*
A. *United Kingdom*						
Gold standard 1881–1913	0.1	2.2	2.7	0.1	2.8	0.8
Floating 1991–2000	3.3	1.1	7.3	0.7	6.6	1.7
B. *United States*						
Gold standard 1881–1913	0.4	3.8	4.4	0.2	4.1	1.4
Floating 1991–2000	2.1	0.5	6.4	0.8	4.7	1.2

Note: This table follows McKinnon, *The International Gold Standard,* 1989.
*The standard deviation of the first differences of annual averages.

The issues raised by how to better manage the volatility of capital flows was the focus of a working group established by the Financial Stability Forum under the chairmanship of Mario Draghi.[1] Its report was published shortly after the March 2000 meeting of the Forum in Singapore.

---

[1] Financial Stability Forum. *Report of the Working Group on Capital Flows.* April 2000.

Should capital flows be regulated?

This report did not in general see tighter control of capital movements as the solution for the problems raised by capital flows. Its basic premise was that the free movement of capital internationally is desirable because it helps both the efficient international allocation of saving among countries and the diversification of risks. But it did recognise that the use of controls on capital *inflows* may be justified for a transitional period in the face of very strong inflows or as countries strengthen the institutional and regulatory environment in their domestic financial systems. In other words, capital controls could be countenanced as prudential measures – often second-best prudential measures. The report did not, however, address the more controversial question of controls on capital *outflows*, largely because such measures are usually elements of crisis management and so were beyond the terms of reference of the Draghi Group.

Is there a case for extending the regulatory framework governing the financial system by adding rules designed to impede capital outflows? This is a controversial question. The consensus view at present is that regulatory arrangements should focus on the riskiness of exposures independently of whether such exposures are primarily domestic or foreign in origin. But this consensus is not universally shared. Several countries in Asia seek to protect themselves against sudden short-term capital outflows by limiting bank lending to non-residents. In many exchange rate crises, pressure on weak currencies has indeed been accentuated by the speculative borrowing of domestic currencies which can then be sold. Hence limiting such bank lending can seem to be an attractive option. However, the experience of many other countries suggests that such limits have become less and less effective in present-day conditions. With the growing internationalisation of business activities – especially through foreign direct investment, which has risen strongly in recent years – the distinction between resident and non-resident becomes ever harder to draw.[1] So too do distinctions between 'legitimate' and 'illegitimate' uses common in exchange control regulations in the past. For instance, a foreign company that has acquired substantial assets in a country and has sizeable business interests can readily find justifications for increasing its borrowing of domestic currency when it wants to 'short' any exposure to the local currency. For these reasons, the case for restricting lending to non-residents in order to deny the potential funding of speculative activity is not overwhelming.

---

[1] Moreover, recent crises have often been fuelled by bona fide residents 'shorting' their own currency.

Managing foreign currency liquidity risks: banks

The main conclusion of the report was that borrowing countries need to have their eyes open to the risks and exposures created by capital inflows. The emphasis is on a proper risk-management strategy for foreign currency liquidity risks. This applies not only to the government's management of its own position (which was extensively discussed in the report) but also to the management of such risks by banks (relevant for this conference).

The report drew lessons for both lending banks (whose loans to emerging markets contributed to an excessive expansion of credit) and for banks in the emerging markets. As regards the former, the report emphasised that lending institutions should be more aware of the risks that they are running, and that fuller disclosure by private institutions was needed in order to strengthen market oversight of lending institutions. Inadequacies in macro-economic data are part of the problem. One obvious weakness concerns data on external debt – in many countries, reporting and statistical systems need to be strengthened to improve the quality of debtor-based data. Until this happens, creditor-based data – largely the BIS banking statistics and data on international bonds – will remain the more reliable source for most countries.

Somewhat less obvious perhaps, but as important, is the need for better statistics on the aggregate exposures of financial institutions. Almost every crisis reveals that the full extent of such exposures is not known at the outset of the crisis – and in some cases true exposures turned out to be much larger than widely believed. The Draghi Report made a number of suggestions about the BIS banking statistics which are being followed up by the relevant central bank committees that meet at the BIS. Extending these statistics is important. This will involve further reporting burdens on banks – who need to be convinced that better data are in their own interest.

The report paid particular attention to risk management by banks in the emerging markets. Shortcomings in this area have made several recent crises much worse. As this report clearly recognises, the work of the Basle Committee in this area has been, and will continue to be, central. The Basle Committee's Core Principles have been key. Their success owes much to the work of a special liaison group – on which developing countries are represented – that provides a forum for discussion and continuous support for supervisors. One important lesson from this experience is that defining standards to be achieved is much more effective when supported by an infrastructure of experienced people. The lesson from this process is that standards and codes work better when set by those who have the best knowledge of and proximity to the matter being considered. No kind of global standard setter would have provided better organisation than the current one, founded on the direct reliance as well as the exercise of consultation and co-ordination.

The IMF and the World Bank have been very closely involved in this work. A central element of the assessments under the joint World Bank/IMF Financial Sector Assessment Program (FSAP) is the monitoring of compliance with the Core Principles. It is difficult to overestimate the importance of these exercises.

Yet additional Basle Committee guidance more specially tailored to the needs of emerging markets may also be needed. It should be remembered that the present trend of supervisory oversight in countries with sophisticated financial institutions and deep financial markets is to rely more on banks' own – often more complex – risk-management procedures. In this world, the supervisors' role is to verify that well-based procedures are in place and to ensure that disclosure is such that the market can sanction excessive risk-taking. One consequence of this trend is that earlier simple supervisory rules or guidelines on particular exposures have fallen into disuse in many highly developed countries.

But such simple rules may still have useful roles to play in the conditions prevailing in many emerging markets. Borrowers in many rapidly developing countries will not have long-established credit histories and this will make credit assessments more difficult. Borrowers in countries that have recently liberalised may not have learnt to deal with foreign exchange risks. The banks and their supervisors may well be inexperienced. In addition, the deep financial markets used for hedging risks in advanced countries may not be available in many emerging markets. (However, the presence of foreign banks raises some additional issues which are considered further below.)

For these reasons, the Draghi Report argued that the liquidity and foreign exchange exposures of banks in some emerging markets could, as an interim measure, be subject to some explicit regulations. Most countries already have rules that limit banks' *net* foreign currency positions. But it is *gross* foreign currency positions that have often proved to be a problem in the past because banks use borrowing in foreign currency – from both foreign banks and domestic foreign currency deposits – to fund domestic loans. In such cases, the banks' net foreign currency exposure may be small because domestic assets denominated in foreign currency 'balance' foreign liabilities. They nevertheless remain exposed to credit risk that arises from their borrowers' foreign exchange risks.

Among the more explicit regulations to limit liquidity and foreign exchange exposures, the Draghi Report listed the following possibilities:

◆ Minimum holdings of liquid foreign assets to cover liquidity risks arising from foreign currency liabilities. Requirements could be tiered so that lower liquidity ratios would apply to long-term foreign currency borrowings than to short-term borrowing.

◆ Reserve requirements, with or without remuneration, could be imposed to discourage foreign currency funding.

◆ Regulations could require banks to match maturities of foreign currency assets and liabilities. More stringent minimum maturities could be imposed on foreign currency funding.

◆ Regulations could require banks to hedge their foreign currency risk exposure in transactions and to ensure that their borrowers hedge their exposure as a condition for obtaining loans from banks.

◆ To lower credit risk, foreign currency loans could be restricted to a fixed percentage of capital or banks could be required to hold more capital and/or loan-loss reserves against these loans.

Over time, more sophisticated approaches to the management of risk should be developed. Large financial institutions have made significant progress in this area in recent years. One trend that deserves emphasis is the development of stress tests. Standard value-at-risk techniques have proved to be of limited value in measuring exposure to extreme market events because: (i) such events occur too rarely to be captured by empirically driven statistical models; and (ii) correlations estimated in normal times change when markets come under stress. A stress test involves the examination of a scenario which is plausible, if somewhat exceptional. A recent BIS review of practice in the private sector found that most private institutions increased the resources they devote to stress tests after the Asian financial crisis in 1997 and the global turbulence in autumn 1998.[1]

Such tests should, in time, help those responsible for financial stability to get a clearer picture of risk intermediation in the financial markets. Although it is too early to know whether the tests applied by individual institutions can be aggregated in a meaningful way (and the difficulties should not be underestimated), the process of asking about the likely consequences of plausible (not of course central) scenarios can be a useful discipline in revealing hidden risks and in ensuring that financial institutions can cope with unexpectedly adverse developments.

---

[1]Committee on the Global Financial System. *Stress testing by large financial institutions: current practice and aggregation issues*. April 2000.

Developing bond markets

A second recommendation of the Draghi Group was the need to develop domestic bond markets. The absence of bond markets has several consequences. The first is that it tends to concentrate intermediation risks on banks, rather than allowing risks to be spread via markets. Alan Greenspan has recently suggested that the banking crises in Asia probably exerted a more depressive impact on activity in the region because of the absence of well-functioning capital markets to take over intermediation that banks with much-weakened balance sheets could not undertake.[1] He argued that the mild US recession of 1991 could have been more severe had not capital markets (which were largely unaffected by the decline in real estate prices) been able to substitute for bank lending.

The second consequence of absent domestic capital markets is that borrowers will tend to incur foreign currency exposures even if the country as a whole has no such exposure. Without capital markets to invest in at home, resident savers have to place their funds abroad and resident investors in effect borrow them back. Where the only funding available in the domestic market is short term (whether from banks or the market), companies which need long-term funding have to choose between borrowing at home (and exposing themselves to maturity risks) and borrowing abroad (foreign exchange risk).[2]

Several emerging market countries are indeed attempting to develop their bond markets. Latin American governments have begun to lengthen the maturity of government debt, which is often short-term or at floating rate. Increased government bond issuance in Asia in the wake of larger budget deficits (inflated by costs of bank restructuring) has begun to create larger bond markets. The absence of fiscal deficits does not necessarily preclude government bond issuance because the authorities can issue debt and invest the proceeds in other assets. But one question with issuing bonds with no deficit to finance is whether governments should in principle take such financial investment decisions, or whether such choices are best left to the private sector. Normally, such decisions are best left to the market; but the social benefits from developing a local bond market may outweigh this. In any event, the volume of outstanding local currency bonds issued by governments in emerging markets has risen substantially in the past decade (see Table 2). Latin American

---

[1] Alan Greenspan. Remarks before the World Bank Group and the IMF. Programme of Seminars, 27 September 1999.

[2] In the absence of long-dated swap markets (can these be very deep without a government bond market?)

issuance has been large (although these figures are inflated by the inclusion of dollar-linked bonds in Argentina and Brazil). There has been a notable rise in the volume of bonds issued in Korea and Thailand (not shown in Table 2).

Table 2. Long-term local debt securities outstanding*
($ billion, at end of year)

	1990	1995	1996	1997	1998	1999
Argentina	6.0	15.7	19.1	23.2	21.7	24.6
Brazil		72.2	96.8	116.2	107.4	112.6
Mexico	23.8	11.2	12.3	14.3	16.9	19.1
Hong Kong	0.4	3.3	2.7	4.1	5.4	6.8
Korea	52.2	114.3	121.6	69.6	137.2	148.5
Malaysia	25.6	40.3	47.	34.5	41.4	52.0
Singapore	25.3	44.7	51.0	11.0	14.2	14.2

* Maturity over one year.
Source: BIS. *International banking and financial market developments.*

However, turnover in such markets remains low. Although statistics on turnover are notoriously unreliable, the turnover ratios recorded in several major emerging market countries is well below the range in most industrial countries (where turnover ratios generally exceed ten). It is possible that low liquidity is an inevitable feature of bond markets in any small country. Bond markets can be liquid only if the different holders have broadly independent liquidity needs. In small countries, domestic holders may tend to need liquidity at the same time (for example during recessions). The presence of foreign holders could offset this to some extent, but such investors may be more subject to herd behaviour. Even so, there are ways of enhancing the liquidity of government bond markets. Several important recommendations were made in a recent note prepared by the Committee on the Global Financial System (CGFS) that meets at the BIS.[1] Included among these were recommendations to concentrate issuance on large benchmark issues at key maturities; to avoid tax distortions that impede liquidity; to ensure transparency; and to develop safe trading and settlement practices.

All this is relatively non-controversial. A more difficult question is whether governments should be even more activist in fostering government debt

---

[1]CGFS (1999). 'How should we design deep and liquid markets: the case of government securities?', October 1999.

markets. One possible policy to support the development of bond markets is to develop funded pension systems. (The poor performance of many government pension schemes suggests that such a policy may well be desirable for its own sake, and indeed this has been advocated by the major international financial institutions.) Given the nature of their future liabilities, such funds tend to invest in government bonds, and many countries have regulations which require investment in domestic securities. The case most often cited is that of Chile, where the development of a local bond market went hand-in-hand with the growth of government-mandated funded pension schemes – and this occurred despite a recent history of high inflation ('original sin' to use Ricardo Hausmann's graphic phrase) that might have made it impossible to build confidence in local currency financial assets.

On the face of it, the simultaneous development of deep government bond markets and extensive funded pension systems seems an attractive combination of policies. But there are three reservations, two of which raise rather fundamental issues. The less fundamental point is that pension funds may simply hold bonds of a given maturity (as long as possible given the maturity of their obligations?) and not trade actively. If so, they might not contribute much to the liquidity of these markets. The second, more fundamental, reservation is that diversification into *foreign* assets is particularly necessary for investors based in small open economies. Investors in such economies should seek to diversify their holdings and not keep too high a proportion of their wealth in domestic assets. This reasoning would argue against pension funds concentrating their investments in domestic assets.[1]

The third reservation relates to the consolidation trend apparently affecting world capital markets. The trading of the equities of emerging market enterprises on the world's largest exchanges has increased. The need for companies to trade their shares in foreign markets gave rise to the ADR market in New York. Companies in emerging markets often prefer listings on big international exchanges because liquidity on the local exchange is too low. Hardly a month goes by without some discussion on the merger on long-standing exchanges.

It is, of course, logically possible to separate the question of the trading of

---

[1] There is, therefore, something of a paradox which arises when the same issue is viewed from assets side as well as the liability side. From the liability side, foreign borrowing exposes the borrower (and sometimes whole economies) to dangerous risks. Yet from the asset side, the accumulation of foreign rather than domestic assets helps savers diversify risks. One resolution of this paradox would be to give up an independent exchange rate – dollarisation, common-currency bloc etc.

different instruments from the issue of different exchanges – different local currency bonds could be traded on the same exchange. But is this entirely plausible? Most financial assets on a given exchange tend to be denominated in a common currency. Such a common currency serves perhaps to broaden the market. Certainly in Europe, the introduction of the euro is often seen as making already-large European bond markets almost as deep and as liquid as that of the US government bond. (Once again the question of independent exchange rate arises.)

Coping with Global Banking Consolidation

The process of consolidation in the financial system globally appears to have strengthened in recent years. Banks world-wide have come under pressure from deregulation, freer trade in financial services and technological innovations. In major countries, the largest banks are becoming bigger – and size is increasingly being seen as necessary for exploiting economies of scale and therefore for maintaining competitive position. In some cases, consolidation has raised questions about the weakening of competition in the banking market.

Banks in emerging markets are likely to face particularly strong pressures. This is partly because many such banks face a high cost of capital or are rather inefficient by world standards. But it is also because of reduced possibilities for diversifying portfolios. In many emerging markets, the scope that local banks have in diversifying risk is inevitably smaller than in larger, more developed economies – because of size, because of more concentrated production and trade or because of concentration on certain markets. Foreign banks, on the other hand, have the advantage of being able to diversify over several different national markets.

The market share of foreign banks in several major emerging market countries has increased sharply in recent years. This has been particularly true in Latin America (see Table 3). Some countries may face the prospect of having largely foreign-owned banking systems in the space of relatively few years. An important issue to resolve is whether the process should be allowed to go as far as this, or does the foreign ownership of the banking system raise issues that do not occur in the foreign ownership of other industries? This is likely to be a complicated and controversial question. It may be useful to distinguish four issues. The first is the nature of competition in the domestic market. Does the behaviour of foreign banks change when they go from having a minority share to having a majority share of the local market? Does the reaction of domestic banks change? Some recent World Bank research which examined various measures of performance of domestic banks found that the entry of foreign banks does indeed make domestic banks more competitive, but this effect depends more on the number of foreign entrants rather than on foreign banks' market share.

Table 3. Share of foreign-owned banks (as a percentage of assets)

	1994	1998	1999
Argentina	22	30	51
Brazil	9	14	23
Chile	20	32	54
Colombia	4	31	26
Mexico	1	18	16

Note: Figures in this table are meant to be indicative only.

In some countries, domestic banks have responded to the threat of increased foreign competition by domestic mergers; and this has on occasion been encouraged by governments. If this is done to increase efficiency (rationalisation), the economy can benefit. But such policies are sometimes driven by a mercantilist keenness to develop 'national champions'. If the new domestic bank that results is large enough to dominate the market and knows the government wants at least one domestic bank to remain viable, competition in the domestic banking market can actually be reduced. A bank that knows it is too big to be taken over may not perform well. Any policy of fostering 'national champions' in the banking industry could serve to create banks that are too big to fail.

The second issue concerns the nature of the supervisory regime to be applied. It was noted above that simple regulations may be useful in supervising banks in some emerging markets. But the trend in the supervision of big international banks is to allow them to use their own risk-management procedures – subject, of course, to both supervisory verification and market discipline. Other banks will still be subject to standardised rules. Applying different standards to domestic and to foreign banks in the same jurisdiction may prove to be something of a challenge, and will inevitably raise level-playing-field issues.

The third issue is how differences in the source of funds affect lending decisions, volatility of lending, etc. The suspicion that foreign banks tend to neglect lending to small businesses is often raised. In addition, foreign banks may draw more funds from abroad, and this can make a difference. What happens, for instance, when foreign banks run into difficulties at home? Do they just pull back even from potentially profitable business abroad? An obvious case for consideration is Japanese bank lending in Asia. Did this fall because of problems in Japan or because of problems in Asian markets?

Finally – and this is perhaps the hardest question to answer – are foreign banks more likely to curtail credit in a crisis? Some research by Federal Reserve Bank of New York economists on the Latin American experience suggests that diversity in ownership appears to contribute to greater stability of credit in times of domestic crises and low domestic demand. If this is true, what can be done to maintain diversity without introducing untoward distortions? Some countries seek to ensure that the foreign owners of local banks come from different countries.

Conclusion

The word 'challenges' which appears in the title of this section of the conference has been used to raise several issues in this paper, while providing few answers. Perhaps one, very tentative, conclusion could be offered. In framing regulatory policies, it is possible that the underlying and long-term forces behind globalisation are being underestimated. Perhaps the eventual result of globalisation will be fewer national banking systems, fewer capital markets and fewer exchange rates. The challenge is to design systems that can be open enough to the potential gains that this process can bring about while guarding against some of the risks.

The Future of the IMF and the World Bank[1]

Montek S. Ahluwalia

The growth of international private capital markets and the increasing access of developing countries to these markets has led some critics to argue that the IMF and the World Bank are no longer needed. This is clearly an extreme view. Despite the growth of private markets it can be argued that both institutions could have important roles to play as producers of global public goods, which cannot be left to markets, and also as instruments for countering various types of market failures.

The Future Role of the IMF

The IMF has the responsibility of overseeing the functioning of the international financial system with a view to ensuring its stability and efficiency. It also promotes sound macro-management in individual member countries which both contributes to stability and is a pre-condition for achieving sustainable growth. To achieve these objectives the Fund relies upon the twin instruments of surveillance and the provision of finance to countries in need. Both functions are likely to remain relevant in future.

Fund surveillance covers bilateral surveillance of individual countries and multilateral surveillance of the world economy. Both types of surveillance have become more important in some respects because globalisation has increased the vulnerability of individual developing countries, and to some extent the international financial system also, to crises.

Bilateral surveillance can, in principle, help reduce the possibility of crises by identifying potential problems at an early stage and encouraging countries to take pre-emptive action. The effectiveness of bilateral surveillance has been criticised in recent years because it failed to give advance warning in many cases, for example in Mexico and East Asia. In the case of Thailand advance warning was given but it was ignored, indicating that surveillance, even when it correctly identifies problems, may not be effective. Despite this experience there is agreement among

---

[1]This contribution is based on *Reforming the Global Financial Architecture* by Montek S. Ahluwalia, published as Economic Paper 41 in the Commonwealth Secretariat Economic Paper series.

both industrialised and developing countries that Fund surveillance is potentially useful and that it should be strengthened.

Bilateral surveillance will become more important in future because of the potential role of financial sector fragility as a cause of crisis in emerging markets and because Fund surveillance can play an important role in identifying such fragility. Much of the discussion of the new financial architecture has focused on the need to upgrade standards in various parts of the financial sector, for example banking, the securities market and insurance, and associated areas such as accounting, bankruptcy legislation and corporate governance. The Fund can play a major role in evolving a consensus on acceptable standards in these areas; it can also encourage emerging market countries to upgrade their standards to these levels.

Multilateral surveillance can also be said to have gained in importance in view of international financial integration because misalignments in industrialised country policies can have major destabilising impacts on international financial markets, imposing heavy costs on developing countries. Developing countries have therefore generally favoured strong multilateral surveillance aimed at achieving better co-ordination of industrialised country policy. One must, however, be realistic about what can be expected from multilateral surveillance in terms of actual impact on industrial country policies.

Experience shows that the multilateral forum is not the most important forum for policy consultation among industrialised countries. The relevant forum for this purpose is really the G-7, where the process of consultations has been institutionalised with an elaborate mechanism for meetings at the level of deputies and regular summit level meetings. Even so, instances of actual policy co-ordination are rare, for example the Plaza and Louvre Accords in the 1980s, and in those cases the Fund was only marginally involved.

Despite these limitations it can be argued that multilateral surveillance is useful because it produces inputs into the G-7 process. This provides a link between the outcome of discussions in multilateral forums, such as the Executive Board of the Fund and the International Monetary and Finance Committee on the one hand, and the more restrictive G-7 groups on the other. It is therefore important to increase the effectiveness of multilateral surveillance, while also ensuring increased participation on the part of developing countries. It is worth considering whether the Fund's input into the G-7 consultation process should be made public.

While the surveillance role of the Fund deals with crisis prevention, it is its financing role that is relevant for crisis resolution and this role is not performed by any other institution. However, there are important differ-ences in perception between developing and industrialised countries on how this role should evolve in future. Developing countries typically argue that the rapid integration of international financial markets, with near instantaneous capital mobility and the ever present dangers of herd-ing and contagion, has greatly increased their vulnerability to crises. The Fund should, therefore, be suitably empowered to help developing coun-tries deal with crisis situations. Industrialised countries recognise that financial integration has increased the possibility of systemic crises and that the Fund has a special responsibility to deal with such crises, but they also worry that the Fund's financing activities have proliferated, often straying beyond the Fund's area of short-term stabilisation into areas that are much more akin to development financing. They also worry that easy access to Fund financing generates moral hazard, weakening the incentives to take preventive action and thus increasing the probability of crises occurring.

There is no doubt that Fund facilities have proliferated in response to the changing needs of its clientele at different points. Some of these have lapsed and some have been recently abolished, but it still has six major facilities.[1] These are the plain vanilla standby arrangements, the Compensatory Financing Facility (CFF), the Extended Fund Facility (EFF), the Poverty Reduction and Growth Facility (PRGF), the Supplemental Reserve Facility (SRF) and the Contingent Credit Line (CCL). These facilities provide very different types of financing, ranging from relatively long-term concessional finance from the PRGF (interest rate of 0.5 per cent and maturity of five and a half to ten years) to very short-term high-cost finance from the SRF (interest rate of 400 to 500 basis points above the standard rate and maturity of 18 months, extend-able by one year).

The Meltzer Commission majority report recommended a drastic restruc-turing which would abolish the present multiple facilities and convert the Fund into a much smaller institution which would act as a quasi-lender of last resort, providing very short-term assistance (120 days with a maxi-mum of one rollover) to solvent emerging economies which meet a set of pre-qualification criteria. The Commission recommended that once pre-

---

[1]Several facilities which used to exist have lapsed, such as the Trust Fund, the Oil Facility, the Structural Adjustment Facility and the Systemic Transformation Facility. More recently, the Buffer Stocking Facility and the Currency Stabilisation Reserve were abolished. The contingency element in the erstwhile Compensatory Contingency Financing Facility (CCFF), which was added at one stage, has also been abolished, converting the facility back into the Compensatory Financing Facility (CFF).

qualification criteria are met, there should be no post-crisis conditionality, except that Fund assistance should not support 'irresponsible budgetary policies'.

The drastic restructuring proposed by the Commission was not unanimous and the majority report has been strongly criticised by a dissenting minority of Commission members. The US Treasury has also indicated to the US Congress that it has fundamental reservations on practically all the main points. The main reasons why the Meltzer Commission's recommendations are unworkable are the following:

◆ Restricting Fund assistance to 'emerging economies' would limit it to around three dozen or so developing and transition countries. It would exclude the overwhelming majority of the membership from eligibility for Fund assistance;

◆ Even if the restrictive reference to 'emerging economies' is eliminated, the vast majority of the Fund's members would still not meet the pre-qualification requirements;

◆ The elimination of post-crisis conditionality puts far too much faith in the process of pre-qualification proposed by the Commission which is limited to the financial sector and the requirement that the government is not following 'irresponsible budgetary policies'. This ignores innumerable other areas of policy where policy imbalances could exist;

◆ The proposal that financing should be limited to 120 days, with a maximum of only one rollover, is far too restrictive even for pure liquidity crises. Crisis-hit countries provided with such short-term financing would be vulnerable to speculation about whether they would be able to meet their obligations at the end of the period.

For all these reasons, restricting the role of the Fund as drastically as proposed by the Meltzer Commission is too extreme a step and could be potentially dangerous. However, it is difficult to deny the need for some further rationalisation. The standby arrangements, the CFF and the EFF should continue. However, the interest rate structure of the EFF could be modified to create an incentive for early repayment. The PRGF, on the other hand, belongs more in the area of the Bank than the Fund and there is a case for shifting this facility to the Bank in a manner which guards against any reduction in the total volume of concessional flows.

The 1990s have seen the emergence of 'new generation' crises which pose new challenges. Unlike traditional crises which originated in a current account deterioration, these crises originate in the capital account. Management of these crises is a new role for the Fund, which is likely to become even more important in future. The financing requirement of such crises is much larger than in traditional episodes of balance of payments diffi- culties and this is especially so since several countries may experience crises simultaneously because of contagion. The Fund must be in a posi- tion to act as a 'lender of last resort' in such cases.

There are interesting differences of perception between industrialised countries and developing countries on this issue. There is general agree- ment that where a crisis is caused primarily by contagion and policy defi- ciencies are not involved, the Fund must aim at providing liquidity, with relatively limited emphasis on conditionality. The CCL was designed to deal with this situation. However, where policy deficiencies are involved, conditionality is unavoidable. The SRF was designed to deal with crises of this type. Experience thus far suggests that both facilities need to be refined in several respects.

The CCL is a potentially innovative instrument but it has not proved suf- ficiently attractive thus far and needs to be made more attractive if it is to be an effective defence against contagion. Since the CCL involves greater pre-crisis discipline, the facility should be made more attractive than the SRF to encourage countries to use it and accept the discipline involved. This could be done if it were made explicit that the scope for post-crisis conditionality in the case of the CCL will be restricted to a narrower area than for the SRF. The extent of automatic disbursement, without imposing new post-crisis conditionality, could be raised from 5 per cent of quota, as at present, to 50 per cent. The interest rate charged for the CCL should also be lower than for the SRF.

The SRF is the principal instrument for managing crises after the event and was used effectively in Korea and Brazil. The design of conditionality in such cases can become a potentially controversial issue as happened in East Asia. It is necessary to ensure that conditionality is sufficiently flex- ible to take account of the specific country situation and does not stray too far from what is needed to ensure stabilisation and restoration of confidence.

An important issue that remains unresolved is the amount of Fund financing that should be made available under the SRF in different cir- cumstances. In principle, it can be argued that once a crisis-hit country has adopted the corrective policies needed to deal with policy deficien- cies, it should be provided with the financing needed to deal with capital outflow, provided it can repay the resources borrowed. However, this means that foreign lenders escape scot-free. There is strong resistance to using public resources from the Fund to finance such outflows, since private creditors should be made to bear some of the costs of imprudent lending. The extent to which private creditors are made to bear part of the burden will obviously depend upon the amount of Fund financing that can be made available; this gives the Fund a critical role in triggering such negotiations.

It is not clear at present how much Fund financing can be made available without forcing some renegotiation with private creditors. One way of introducing transparency would be to establish objective norms for the amount of financing, as a multiple of quota that would be available to support adjustment without insisting on debt restructuring. Countries that are able to manage within this limit without restructuring would be allowed to do so. However, if financing was needed beyond this amount, it would only be provided if parallel action was taken by the country to negotiate with private creditors. This approach has the advantage of transparency, but it may not be the best approach. The financing need in a crisis varies greatly for reasons beyond a country's control and a more flexible approach, determining the limits of financing on the basis of individual cases, may be better. The issue of the degree of transparency to be adopted is difficult to resolve.

Managing new generation crises also raises the issue of the resources that must be put at the Fund's disposal. In many crises the Fund has had to supplement its own resources with resources from other bilateral donors, the World Bank and the regional development banks. The need to tap other sources inevitably introduces uncertainty and non-uniformity in the extent of financial support that can be provided in different situations. The Fund's credibility as a multilateral crisis manager requires that it should have sufficient access to resources under its own control to manage crises when they arise. This suggests the need to consider establishing a special mechanism, based on the creation of SDRs, which could provide the Fund with adequate resources for use in emergency situations, subject to majority decision of the Fund Board.

The Role of the World Bank

The Bank performs three different types of functions, each of which will remain relevant in the future: it serves as a conduit for long-term concessional assistance, through the International Development Association (IDA), to low-income countries; it acts as an intermediary providing non-concessional loans to creditworthy developing countries; and it engages in research and provides advice on development policy. Assessment of its future role must depend upon assessment of the role of each of these functions.

The role of the Bank as a conduit for IDA flows to the poorest countries remains essential for the task of reducing global poverty, an objective which is regarded as a global public good. This role is particularly important in the low-income countries of sub-Saharan Africa, where growth rates have been very low in the 1980s and 1990s and where a significant improvement in growth or acceleration of poverty reduction is not possible without additional concessional assistance.

The role of the Bank as an intermediary for non-concessional flows is more open to question in view of the development of capital markets. However, there are strong arguments in favour of a continuing role for Bank lending.

◆ A large number of developing countries do not have significant access to capital markets and depend almost exclusively on the International Bank for Reconstruction and Development (IBRD) lending for non-concessional loans.

◆ Many countries that do have substantial access would not find it possible to completely replace borrowing from the Bank by private financing without a significant deterioration in their credit rating. Private markets will not provide finance on long maturities as is available from the Bank, and a shift to private financing will therefore imply a deterioration in the debt structure with a reduction in borrowing capacity.

◆ Private capital markets are highly volatile and developing countries are poorly placed to handle such volatility. The active involvement of the Bank provides an element of stability in capital flows, and possibly also the possibility of counter-cyclical action.

◆ Continued access to Bank lending for countries which could otherwise obtain resources from private markets can be justified on the grounds that it can influence the allocation of resources in a desirable direction. For example, Bank lending directed at sectors such as health, education or environmental protection can ensure a larger flow of resources to these sectors than would occur if the government borrowed from private markets because the latter would generate funds that are much more fungible.

◆ Finally, Bank lending can be used for leverage in policy reforms in many infrastructure sector areas which in many developing countries have traditionally been dominated by the public sector, but which could attract large volumes of private sector investment if the necessary reforms are implemented. This is a potentially important role for Bank lending which private lenders will not play. This is, in fact, a very useful development role which the Bank can play in countries which have market access. Far from substituting for private lending, Bank lending in such cases can actually lay the framework for future growth of private investment and reliance on private capital.

In recent years the Bank has also emphasised its new role, based on its research activities and the experience gained from its economic and sector work in many countries, of providing 'knowledge inputs' into development. This is undoubtedly an important activity, especially since development objectives have become much more multi-dimensional (growth, poverty alleviation, access to basic social services, gender imbalance removal, participation, sustainability, etc.) and the range of policies considered relevant for development has also widened considerably. However, it is relevant to ask whether the activity of disseminating knowledge should be unconnected with Bank lending. In practice, however, effectiveness of transmission depends critically upon its being combined with a substantial volume of lending from the Bank. The decline in the volume of IBRD lending in recent years, after adjusting for lending in support of IMF crisis management packages, is a disturbing development from this point of view, and needs to be reversed.

A related issue is that the accumulation of knowledge as the multi-faceted nature of development objectives and policies should not lead to over-crowing of conditionality. The Bank's ability to perform the role of leveraging policy in desired directions depends upon its ability to limit excessive conditionality which burdens each loan or programme with multiple concerns. Bank financing has the advantages of low interest rates and long maturity. But an excessive load of conditionality can add to the hassle factor associated with Bank lending; this will have the effect of reducing the willingness of developing countries to absorb Bank funding, and thus limit the Bank's ability to leverage policy reform.

The Role of the IMF: A Guide to the Reports

John Williamson

Introduction

Many of the discussions on a new international financial architecture that were spawned by the East Asian crisis have dealt with the future role of the IMF. This paper starts by summarising the recommendations of five recent reports and one speech, and the reasoning that lies behind them. The recommendations are divided into four main areas: (i) the scope of Fund activities; (ii) surveillance; (iii) lending; and (iv) governance (on which topic a recent academic paper is also summarised). The last section of the paper offers a verdict on the first three of these topics.

The first of the five reports considered was published jointly by the International Centre for Monetary and Banking Studies in Geneva and the Centre for Economic Policy Research (CEPR) in London. The authors were Jose De Gregorio, Barry Eichengreen, Takatoshi Ito and Charles Wyplosz (1999). The report also contains brief accounts of alternative reform proposals made by Kiichi Miyazawa, Jeffrey Sachs, Sebastian Edwards, France, the UK and Italy, and of the idea of regional funds. It was discussed at a conference held in Geneva in May 1999, which is also reported in the document. This paper will be referred to as the Geneva Report.

The second report is that of an independent task force sponsored by the Council on Foreign Relations (CFR) and published in 1999. The task force was jointly chaired by Carla Hills and Peter Peterson, with Morris Goldstein as Project Director and 23 other luminaries of the American internationalist establishment, including C. Fred Bergsten, Director of the Institute for International Economics (IIE), as members. This will be referred to as the CFR Report. It contains eight statements of dissenting views, but all members signed the main report.

The third report was commissioned by the G-24 and written by Montek Ahluwalia in 1999. It was published by the United Nations Conference on Trade and Development (UNCTAD) in the latest volume of its series of publications of G-24 studies. It will be referred to as the Ahluwalia Report.

The fourth report is that of the International Financial Institution [sic]

Advisory Commission (IFIAC), established by the US Congress and chaired by Allan Meltzer, with an additional ten members including academics Charles Calomiris, Jerome Levinson and Jeffrey Sachs, businessmen, politicians, and think-tank directors C. Fred Bergsten of the IIE and Edwin Feulner of the Heritage Foundation. Despite the singular 'Institution' in its title, the report's terms of reference covered the World Bank, the three regional development banks, the WTO and the BIS, as well as the IMF. This was issued in March 2000 and will be referred to as the IFIAC report. It was accompanied by two 'supporting statements' arguing that it did not go far enough in gutting the IFIs, a joint minority statement by four members (including Bergsten and Levinson), three of whom did not sign the main report, and two additional dissents by two members of the minority (one of whom was Levinson) who did not sign the main report.

The fifth report is that of a task force established by the Overseas Development Council (ODC) in Washington, which reported in April 2000. This was co-chaired by John Sewell and Sylvia Saborio, directed by Kevin Morrison and comprised a further 11 members from academia, think-tanks, and non-governmental organisations 'who agreed with the overall direction and recommendations of the report, but not necessarily with all statements and emphases'. Task force members included Nancy Birdsall, Joe Stiglitz and John Williamson. This will be referred to as the ODC Report.

The speech included is that given by US Secretary of the Treasury Lawrence Summers at the London Business School in December 1999.

These six works include the views advanced by an international group of academics, by a collection of Americans who qualify as 'the great and the good', by a leading developing country official writing on behalf of the Group of 24 developing countries, by a mixed group of Americans writing a report for the US Congress, by another mixed group of predominantly American composition concerned with the problems of developing countries, and by the US Secretary of the Treasury. Although there is obviously some bias toward American sources, this provides a reasonable cross-section of informed thought on which to develop a set of proposals.

The Scope of the IMF

Not all the six documents being surveyed address all four of the topics discussed in this paper. The desirable scope of IMF activities, for example, is not touched on by the Geneva Report.

The CFR Report also treats the topic relatively cursorily, but it does urge the Fund (and, for that matter, the World Bank) to go 'back to basics'. It argues (p. 115) that the Fund is still needed to help countries resolve payments problems in an internationally responsible way, to address liquidity crises and to act as a crisis manager or convenor. Elsewhere it emphasises the Fund's role in crisis prevention. It also argues that 'the IMF is losing its focus and reducing its effectiveness by doing too much. Specifically, the IMF should limit the scope of its conditionality to monetary, fiscal, exchange rate and financial-sector policies' (p. 116). But it argues that the Fund's surveillance needs to be concerned with monitoring compliance with financial standards, as well as macro fundamentals.

The Ahluwalia Report (p. 22) dismisses the case for a merger between the Fund and the Bank on the grounds that there is an important and distinctive role for the Fund in dealing with crises, both in prevention (via surveillance) and in management (via financing). The report also argues that 'such financing does not have to be long-term and certainly not concessional'. It also states: 'The Fund should focus more sharply on sources of instability in the international financial system and on handling balance-of-payments problems which are either short-term or systemic in nature'. It goes on to suggest: 'It could even be argued that financing operations related to chronic balance-of-payments problems of low-income countries, e.g. the Enhanced Structural Adjustment Facilities (ESAF) and Heavily Indebted Poor Countries initiative should perhaps be shifted to the Bank, with co-operation from the Fund being available on technical matters'.

The Executive Summary of the IFIAC Report declares that 'the IMF should continue as crisis manager under new rules that give member countries incentives to increase the safety and soundness of their financial systems' (p. 6). The report identifies three roles implied by this: (i) serving as quasi-lender of last resort to emerging economies; (ii) collecting, publishing, and disseminating data on member countries; and (iii) providing advice (as opposed to imposing conditionality) relating to economic policy (pp. 42–43). It urges an end to long-term loans and specifically calls for the closing of what it calls the 'poverty and growth facility' (p. 43). It also calls for the replacement of conditionality by pre-qualification, according to principles outlined in the section on lending below.

The CFR Report argues that 'the IMF is losing its focus and reducing its effectiveness by doing too much . . .'

The ODC Report identifies the IMF's core competence as macroeconomic policy and hence sees its central role as crisis avoidance and, when that fails, promoting speedy recovery from crisis. It argues that this implies that its lending should be restricted to short-term liquidity lending in macro-economic crises, and calls for the Poverty Reduction and Growth Facility (PRGF) to be moved to the World Bank. It argues that the Fund should retain a role in the poorest countries, but only in the context of emergency lending, as in other member countries. The Fund should maintain its role in surveillance, geared toward providing advice that would minimise the probability of crises. But the report argues that statistics should be collected and disseminated by an independent statistical agency, rather than by the Fund (or Bank).

The Summers speech also urges a focus on core competence (p. 5), but it interprets this rather more widely than the preceding reports. It suggests that the IMF should promote financial stability within countries, a stable flow of capital between them and rapid recovery following any financial disruption (p. 3). Summers asserts that this points to six critical areas:

♦ promoting the flow of information from governments to markets and investors;

♦ giving attention to financial vulnerability as well as macro-economic fundamentals;

♦ developing a more selective financing role focused on emergency situations;

♦ catalysing market-based solutions;

♦ focusing on growth and poverty reduction in the poorest countries;

♦ modernising the IMF as an institution.

The degree of consensus reflected in these five sources is rather remarkable. All reflect a concern with mission creep, and urge the Fund to focus on its core competence. All see the Fund as having a central role in aiming to prevent financial crises, and in managing them when they nevertheless occur. All wish the Fund to continue to lend in crisis situations. All concur in wishing to maintain surveillance, and none challenge the proposition that this should focus on financial standards and vulnerability as well as traditional macro-economic fundamentals.

Despite the apparent agreement, there is a profound gulf between the IFIAC majority, on the one hand, and the other five (together with the IFIAC minority), on the other, about the value of having an IMF at all. Everyone except the IFIAC majority emphasises the need for an international institution dedicated to building collaborative macro-economic policies among countries, to helping avoid crises and to aiding countries cope with crises that nonetheless occur. They all appear to agree that the world is a lot better off for having built that degree of international collaboration. The IFIAC majority starts instead from a concern that IMF lending may promote moral hazard (a phenomenon whose importance 'cannot be overstated'[1]), and concedes only reluctantly (and to the dismay of two of their number) that there may, after all, be a limited role for the Fund. On more concrete issues the disputed topics would seem to be:

◆   whether the Fund should maintain the PRGF (Summers considers that it should);

◆   whether the PRGF should be closed (IFIAC majority report) or moved to the Bank (Ahluwalia and ODC);

◆   whether the collection and dissemination of statistics should be moved to a separate agency, as urged by ODC.

Surveillance

Fund surveillance takes two forms: (i) general surveillance of the world economy, as reflected in the biennial publication *World Economic Outlook* and the annual *International Capital Markets Report*; and (ii) surveillance of individual countries, as undertaken primarily in Article IV consultations. No-one appears to challenge the usefulness of the former exercise or to offer significant suggestions for improving what the Fund does, except the Ahluwalia Report which urges that the Fund should draw on this information in introducing developing country interests into G-7 discussions. The debate focuses rather on surveillance of individual countries, and how this could be improved to diminish the probability of crises occurring.

The Geneva Report suggests that surveillance should seek to identify country vulnerabilities in areas like the banking system, exchange rate policy, reserve levels or accounting standards, and give countries confidential warnings of these vulnerabilities. It recognises that the Fund lacks expertise in many of the fields where standards are needed and being developed, and urges the Fund to accept that the standards will be designed by others, with its own role being confined to monitoring, with the use of experts from other institutions in its missions.

The CFR Report also suggests that the Fund should focus on each member country's compliance with international financial standards like the Fund's Special Data Dissemination Standard, the Basle Committee's Core Principles of Effective Banking Supervision and international accounting

[1]Prompting Paul Krugman (2000) to quip 'Oh, yes it can!'

standards, along with a 'viable' exchange rate regime, prudent debt management, etc. Rather than the results being communicated confidentially, however, the report proposes that the Fund should periodically publish a 'standards report' that details each country's performance, along with the Article IV reports assessing policies and prospects. It sees the incentive to comply with these standards as being provided by the likelihood of a lower cost of market borrowing, cheaper access to Fund credit when a country has to borrow and lower capital requirements for bank loans to those countries (pp. 93–97). The Fund should encourage countries with fragile domestic financial sectors and weak prudential frameworks to adopt Chilean-style capital inflow taxes (p. 98).

The Ahluwalia Report declares that surveillance is a core activity of the Fund and recommends that it be strengthened, primarily by increasing the disclosure of key information to financial markets.

The IFIAC Report has rather little to say about surveillance, except that the Fund should abandon Article IV consultations for the OECD countries (on the grounds of avoiding costly duplication of effort) and should publish promptly all Article IV consultation reports for other countries (pp. 43–44). It also sees a major function of the Fund as being the collection and prompt publication of data, with a view to keeping market participants well informed (p. 43). It proposes that the Fund should encourage countries either to hard fix their exchange rate or to float, since intermediate regimes are more subject to crises.

The ODC Report also approves of data collection (though arguing that this should be moved to a separate agency) and transparency, but argues that improvement in these directions is unlikely to end crises. It sees a unique role for the Fund in advising countries on macro policy aimed, *inter alia*, at avoiding macro-economic crises, and normally not based on financial arrangements. It too endorses Fund monitoring of a wide range of standards, while cautioning that the Fund does not have in-house expertise on all of them. It recommends that discussion of Article IV reports be moved from the full Executive Board to the sub-boards comprised of the executive directors (EDs) from particular geographical regions of the world, so as to diminish the workload on the full Board, but with regular reports from the sub-boards to the full Board. The report cautions against enthusiasm for the two-corners exchange rate fad (the notion that every country ought to have either a currency board or a floating exchange rate, but nothing in between).

Secretary Summers also favours a Fund role in collecting and disseminating information to investors and markets. Countries should be encouraged to adopt the SDDS and the various international codes that are being developed for sound policies, and the Fund's assessment of their compliance with those standards should be released into the public domain. Surveillance should cover financial vulnerability as well as macro fundamentals, and it should be recognised that this vulnerability is a function of the level of short-term foreign debt and of excessive government granting of guarantees. The Fund should focus on the strength of national balance sheets, for example by developing a more meaningful measure of reserve adequacy than the traditional reserves/imports ratio. It should draw attention to 'the dangers of opening up to short-term capital in the presence of too many domestic guarantees', and should highlight the risks posed by unsustainable exchange rate regimes.

Once again, the degree of consensus exhibited is quite significant. There is general enthusiasm for data collection (if not necessarily by the Fund), transparency, publication and continued surveillance. This is rather remarkable if one considers how secretive an institution the Fund has traditionally been. Several of the sources explicitly endorse focusing attention on vulnerabilities in the financial system, foreign debt, the various areas in which international standards are being promulgated and the exchange rate regime, and no-one opposes this approach. There was far greater recognition of a possible constructive role for capital inflow taxes than one would have expected to find in these places prior to the East Asian crisis. There remains a disagreement as to whether all intermediate exchange rate regimes are to be condemned as unsustainable, but everyone recognises that the issue of sustainability is an important one.

Lending

The Geneva Report expresses scepticism about the proposal to 'include some form of "pre-qualification" for financial support by the IMF' (p. 44).[1] It sees the appeal of pre-qualification as lying in a resolution of the problem of moral hazard, since a government could no longer be expected to be bailed out if it ignored warnings of imprudent behaviour. But it questions whether government moral hazard is a real problem (governments suffer enough when they engulf their countries in a crisis to eliminate any incentive to flirt with danger), and also argues that the criteria for pre-qualification would be arbitrary and the policy would be time-inconsistent (the threat to withhold help from countries that have no pre-qualified is not credible). The report also declares that the CCL created by the IMF in April 1999 suffered from the same drawbacks, as

---

[1] However, it did suggest lower interest rates on Fund lending to countries that include collective action clauses in their bond contracts, a related suggestion that is pursued later in this paper.

well as from the danger that disqualifying a country previously qualified could precipitate a crisis. It notes that no country has so far been induced to apply for a CCL.

The Geneva Report also argues that the Fund's facilities have proliferated excessively and need to be streamlined with a view to making the Fund's emergency lending more transparent, simple and effective (p.48). It applauds the new SRF (which can lend exceptionally large sums at a penalty interest rate and was first deployed in South Korea) as a step in the right direction (p.53). It argues that the capital account crises that are now dominant are essentially caused by a lack of liquidity rather than bad fundamentals, and therefore require temporary financing with front-loaded disbursements (though it questions whether the support need always be large). Support from the Fund will need to be accompanied either by 'co-financing with the private-sector rollovers and rescheduling' or by a restructuring of external debt obligations in order to keep the size of financial packages within reason. The experience of South Korea in 1997 showed that a standstill could be a useful instrument in bailing in the private sector, but the experience of Mexico in 1982 should also stand as a warning that standstills are not a panacea.

The CFR Report proposes to draw a sharp distinction between 'country crises' and 'systemic crises'. Finance for the former would be limited to normal access limits (100 per cent of quota per year and 300 per cent cumulatively), and would be financed from the Fund's existing resources. Systemic crises might be financed from the General Arrangements to Borrow (GAB) and the New Arrangements to Borrow (NAB), or from a proposed new Contagion Facility that would replace both the CCL and the SRF. The Contagion Facility would be used for victims of contagion in which the payments deterioration reflected developments largely beyond their own control and would not require a Fund programme (p.110). It would be financed by a one-off SDR allocation in which all Fund members would donate their newly allocated SDRs to the Contagion Facility. The report also declares that in extreme cases, where the debt profile is clearly unsustainable, the Fund should require debtors to engage in 'good-faith' debt restructuring negotiations with their credi-tors as a condition of its support (p.102). Those discussions might be facilitated by declaration of a temporary standstill by the debtor. Interest rates on borrowings from the Fund would be lower for countries that made a series of efforts to forestall crises by complying with the inter-national codes being developed, following sound macro policies, main-taining a viable currency regime and a prudent debt profile, and estab-lishing contingent sources of liquidity support (p.94).

The Ahluwalia Report is sympathetic to the Fund acting as a lender of last resort in response to capital account crises, but worries about how such lending is to be financed. It also suggests resorting to a special SDR allocation (p.14), as well as to bigger quotas. In terms of conditionality for such lending, it is sympathetic to pre-qualification but points to the problem that performance criteria judged adequate prior to a crisis may not appear to be so after the crisis has erupted (p.16). It suggests a compromise solution in which pre-qualification would entitle a country to a first tranche almost automatically, but subsequent drawings would require conditionality. It notes the danger that withdrawal of cover before a crisis could precipitate a loss of confidence that would provoke the very crisis that the arrangement was designed to avoid.

The IFIAC Report identifies the first of the Fund's responsibilities as being 'to act as a quasi-lender of last resort to solvent emerging economies' (p.42). The first point to note is that this is the only lending window that the report discusses; it appears to preclude not just lending to industrial countries, but also to the poorer developing countries that are not included in the term 'emerging economies'. Indeed, it specifically calls for closing the PRGF, currently the main instrument for lending to those countries (p.43), and it rules out lending for non-financial emergencies, such as famines (p.47). The report goes on to state that 'except in unusual circumstances, where the crises poses [sic] a threat to the global economy, loans would be only to countries in crises [sic] that have preconditions that establish financial soundness' (p.43). Preconditions would replace conditionality. The preconditions proposed (pp.44–45) are:

◆ freedom of entry and operation for foreign financial institutions;

◆ well-capitalised commercial banks, preferably with part of the capital in the form of uninsured subordinated debt;

◆ regular and timely publication of the maturity structure of outstanding sovereign and guaranteed debt and off-balance sheet liabilities;

◆ 'a proper fiscal requirement', the nature of which is not specified.

Countries that need to borrow before they have been able to fulfil these conditions should be entitled to do so at a 'super penalty rate' (all borrowing would be at a penalty rate), and countries that choose not to fulfil the conditions should be ineligible to borrow (p.46). These loans would be of short maturity (for example a maximum of 120 days) with only one allowable rollover. The report also goes to considerable length to ensure the priority of IMF claims over all other claims, in analogy with the requirement of collateral in traditional last-resort lending.

Perhaps the most important criticism voiced by the minority who did not sign the IFIAC Report concerns the proposed limitations on borrowing from the Fund. They question whether it would be possible to fashion a fiscal pre-qualification requirement that would dispense with the need for conditionality, and are also concerned that the pre-qualification approach might preclude lending to countries of great systemic importance (pp. 121–22). They commend instead the CFR proposal to grant preferential lending terms to countries that have adopted the Basle Core Principles to strengthen their domestic banking systems (pp. 123–24).[1]

The ODC Report also sees the Fund's lending role as driven by crisis management, but it states explicitly that all countries should be eligible to borrow from the Fund in times of macro-economic crisis (p. 6). In furtherance of the objective of cutting back the IMF to its core competence, which excludes structural issues, it proposes to abolish the EFF and to transfer the PRGF (and hence also responsibility for the Heavily Indebted Poor Countries programme) from the Fund to the Bank. The Fund should advise the Bank on the macro conditions to be required for PRGF loans, though without a veto. The report argues that crisis lending should be done through the use of normal standby arrangements, which should be accessible by any member country, with a subsidised interest rate when one of the low-income members borrows. Conditionality should revert to focusing on the basics of macro policy, without the addition of numerous structural conditions such as adorned the East Asian programmes which, in the event, proved almost entirely irrelevant to nurturing the region's rapid recovery from crisis. The report calls for an effort to make *ex ante* assessments of the impact of IMF programmes on the poor, with a view to trying to reduce their adverse impact. It expresses scepticism about the CCL but calls for maintenance of the CFF.

Secretary Summers also calls for the Fund to focus its financing on emergency situations. It should be a last, not a first, resort; a backstop, not an alternative, to private finance. Longer-term lending would be phased out and the core instruments would become the CCL, short-term stand-by arrangements for countries with non-systemic problems and the SRF for systemic capital account crises. He argues that the penalty rate

---

[1] At a meeting at the Brookings Institution on 11 April 2000, Alan Meltzer claimed that the majority report also contains just such a proposal for discriminating between lending at a penalty rate to countries that had pre-qualified ('List A') and lending at a super penalty rate to the rest ('List B'). There does not appear to be any passage in the majority report that bears that interpretation, beyond the transitional period, but his claim may be interpreted as indicating that at least the chairman of the Commission has been intellectually convinced of the desirability of this approach.

on SRF lending is a precedent on which to build, although the CCL might have a lower interest rate to encourage countries to qualify and apply. Conditionality will have to fit the specific country circumstances, but it should not intrude in areas irrelevant to the restoration of stability and growth. However, 'the stability of banking systems, issues of social cohesion and inclusion, and the capacity to enforce contractual arrangements' may all be relevant (p. 6). He also urges the official sector to help creditors to recognise their collective interest in maintaining exposure, even when their individual interest is in withdrawing funds. It will, however, occasionally be necessary to seek less voluntary debt restructuring and, in exceptional cases, the IMF should be prepared to lend into arrears.

In his remarks on the poorest countries (p. 8), Summers lauds the progress made in developing the HIPC as 'a fundamentally new framework for the international community's efforts to combat poverty, one that gives the World Bank the lead and the IMF a more tightly focused role'. He does not hint at the desirability of moving the PRGF.

The common theme of these six sources is the central role of IMF financing in managing crises. There are clearly a number of other ideas that have appealed quite widely without achieving unanimous support: some form of pre-qualification (though with a strategic difference as to whether failure to pre-qualify would disqualify a country from borrowing or simply stiffen the terms); shifting the PRGF from the Fund to the Bank; and accompanying IMF crisis lending by some form of payments standstill, at least in certain circumstances.

Governance

The Geneva Report argues that the IMF needs greater transparency and more accountability. More decisions should be taken by vote rather than consensus, and the minutes and the votes should be published. Programmes should be evaluated both by staff and by outside panels, and the findings should be published. Above all, the Executive Board should become independent in the same sense that the boards of many central banks are now independent; they should be appointed for multi-year terms and should not receive instructions from the governments that appointed them, the Board should be given an explicit mandate such as promoting economic and financial stability, and the Board should periodically report to what is now the International Monetary and Financial Committee (the IMFC, formerly known as the Interim Committee). A country under discussion should send a representative to sit with the Board. In order to increase its independence from governments, the Fund should borrow in the market rather than acquire its resources from member governments.

The CFR Report also urges more transparency, but Fund governance is not prominent among its concerns. Likewise the Ahluwalia Report says little on this topic, except for arguing against a merger of the Fund and the Bank, and suggesting the establishment of an overarching ministerial committee to supervise them both. The IFIAC Report calls for the Fund to be restructured as a smaller institution (p. 42), and for more transparency in its accounting (pp. 50–51).

The ODC Report calls for a realignment of the voting power in the Fund to reflect the current weight of economic power; this would involve Asian representation growing and that of Europe diminishing. The report recommends reducing the super-majority needed for certain key decisions so as to eliminate the US veto. It also calls for a more neutral and transparent process for the selection of the managing director. It recommends that the links between member countries and the Fund should be broadened, so that the Fund could interact with a prime minister's office or a planning ministry (or, in developed countries, an overseas aid ministry), rather than just with the finance ministry and central bank. It urges the establishment of a small external evaluation unit to report to the IMFC. (The Fund announced the establishment of such a permanent evaluation office just days before the report was published, but reporting to the Executive Board rather than to the IMFC.) The report also urges that data collection and dissemination should be relocated to a separate statistical agency.

It is difficult to detect much common ground between these proposals, beyond the general desire to continue to advance in the direction of greater transparency and openness, although it might be possible to find a widespread desire to reform the process of selecting the Managing Director after the recent fiasco. Perhaps it is premature to try to reform the Fund's governance before it has been decided what the Fund should do.[1]

---

[1]Nevertheless, there may be some interest in a set of proposals in a recent article that focused exclusively on the question of Fund governance (Askari and Chebil, 1999). They express concern about the distribution of quotas, and the ad hoc procedures for adjusting quotas, which have led to current anomalies like the large over-representation of Euroland and Saudi Arabia and the under-representation of South Korea, and arguably China, and a number of other Asian countries. They recommend reducing the super-majority needed to approve certain decisions so as to deprive the USA of its veto, citing the conditionality that Congress has unilaterally imposed on the Fund for its approval of quota increases as intolerable for a multilateral institution.

An Agenda for Reform of the IMF

At this stage this paper will discuss what an agenda for the reform of the IMF might look like. It will not address the issues of governance, since one first needs to decide what the Fund should do. The paper is in full agreement with the consensus views on the scope of the Fund that were noted earlier. In particular, it endorses the view that the failure to resist the mission creep imposed on it by the G-7, and most specifically the conditionality that the US Congress attached to the most recent increase in Fund quotas, threatens to undermine the effectiveness of the IMF. The Fund should indeed return to concentrate on its core competence. There seems to be unanimous agreement about what that is (at least among those who do not dismiss the IMF as irreparably incompetent). For example, the G-7 communiqué of 15 April 2000 stated: 'Crisis prevention and response should be at the core of the IMF's work'. Everyone seems to agree that that involves both maintaining surveillance, with a view to avoiding crises, and helping to manage those crises which nevertheless occur.

It is extraordinary that the official world, including Secretary Summers and those who endorsed the decisions of the spring meetings of the IMFC, regard these principles as consistent with the maintenance of the PRGF (and therefore with the HIPC, whose conditionality is tied to the PRGF) in the Fund. It is one thing to oppose the recommendation of the

---

(This included in 1989 a requirement that the Fund recruit development economists trained in analysing the linkages between macro-economic conditions and short- and long-term impacts on sustainable management of natural resources, and in 1998 a requirement that no IMF money be used to subsidise South Korean industries that compete with US industries (see Askari and Chebil, 1999, p.351)). They advance a number of proposals for improving the operation of the Executive Board: seeking a greater diversity of backgrounds of Executive Directors, and even appointing a couple of non-voting Directors with no country affiliation from the private sector; making all the constituencies multi-country; and encouraging the Board to initiate proposals rather than simply rubber-stamp staff initiatives. They argue that the positions of the Managing Director and First Deputy Managing Director should be opened up to the best person available, irrespective of nationality and professional background, and again betray a sympathy for candidates from the private financial sector. They urge that the staff should also have more diverse professional backgrounds than economists with PhDs from American universities, and that there should be higher rewards for good performers and a greater willingness to fire poor performers. They criticise the use of the IMF as a political slush fund (a theme that can also be found in several of the five reports that have been reviewed, although not in the speech of Secretary Summers). They argue for transparency and point to deficiencies in the Fund's historical record on corruption. They conclude that the time has come for a comprehensive review of the IMF's governance in parallel with its policies, and urge the Fund's management to reach out to international civil society in initiating a review which might strengthen the Fund and enhance its performance.

IFIAC majority to close the PRGF,[1] which would imply reducing the resource transfer to the poorest countries. But both the Ahluwalia and ODC reports suggested an alternative – not closing it but, rather, transferring it to the Bank. The argument for this is that the PRGF is not concerned with crisis lending, the area of the Fund's core competence, but with poverty reduction and growth. No-one doubts that growth, and the poverty reduction that flows from it, is critically dependent upon disciplined macro policies, and that these lie within the core competence of the Fund. But macro policy is, as emphasised in the Bank's Comprehensive Development Framework, merely one of a number of areas that it is essential to get roughly right if an economy is to grow at anything close to its potential rate. Since the Bank has the core competence in most of these fields, it seems quixotic to place the PRGF in the Fund rather than the Bank. This is an anomaly that can be explained only by history.[2]

Quixotic it may seem, but the location of the PRGF in the Fund has been vigorously defended by Stanley Fischer in his capacity as the IMF's Acting Managing Director. As quoted in the *Financial Times* on 14 April 2000, he said, in response to a question about the recommendation to move the PRGF in the ODC report:

> there is no reason poor countries should not be able to benefit from the IMF's expertise in macro-economic policy. The argument strikes me as one which imagines there is a different macro-economics for poor countries and rich countries. Inflation and economic [in]stability is bad for all people.

This misinterprets the ODC report, which explicitly argues (p. 5) that the Fund has 'a unique role in the international system, including in poor countries: to advise countries on how to avoid macro-economic crisis and to restore stability in the midst of such crises'. The ODC report also says baldly: 'Stability is an essential condition for growth'. In fact, the argument is one for eliminating the differential treatment of poor and rich countries in all respects except one: the interest rate at which they are entitled to borrow should they need to borrow in the event of a macro

---

[1] However, members of the IFIAC majority have in private conversation urged that one should not take the text of the report too literally, and stated they would not oppose transferring the PRGF to the Bank.

[2] Specifically, the IMF was allowed to sell a small part of its gold holdings in the 1970s, after the monetary use of gold was first suppressed, in order to create a trust fund to make low-interest loans to poor countries. In the late 1970s, the Fund also made extensive standby loans to poor countries, which they were unable to service in the adverse conditions of the 1980s. Both were therefore refinanced by low-interest loans from a newly-created Structural Adjustment Facility in the 1980s, which was further expanded to the Enhanced Structural Adjustment Facility in the 1990s. This was renamed the PRGF in 1999 to reflect the increased concern with poverty.

crisis. The Fund would retain the same role in both types of countries, namely surveillance directed to crisis avoidance and short-term lending when avoidance fails. Perhaps there is a good argument for retaining the PRGF in the Fund but, if so, Fischer did not articulate it.[1] Of course, he would have jeopardised his reputation as an outstanding bureaucrat had he acknowledged the logic of transferring a substantial part of his organisation's responsibilities to its sibling institution. One can hardly expect him to spearhead this particular reform, but that does not make it an undesirable change.

The danger of locating the facility in the Fund is that its traditions will prevent it from treating macro policy as merely one among a number of critical areas. On past experience one has to expect that the Fund will always make macro stability *primus inter pares*, whether it deserves to be or not. However, when countries are not in crisis, macro stability ought not to be accorded primacy. If the Fund is in charge, there will be no-one to countermand an excessive emphasis on macro perfection at the expense of getting public expenditure priorities right and reforming corporate governance and building up the education system. If the Bank is in charge, the Fund will still have the duty to examine macro policy and will be able to make a case if it sees problems; if the Bank agrees that macro stability is in jeopardy then it will have the duty to hold up disbursement until policy has been adjusted appropriately. This will ensure both that the Fund cannot be ignored and that countries cannot be deprived of its advice. But since another agency will have to agree that macro stability is indeed at risk, the country will be safeguarded against an excessive emphasis on macro stability at the expense of other priorities.

The other argument for relocating the PRGF concerns the time horizon of Fund programmes. We know that poverty reduction requires decades, rather than the three years allotted to a PRGF programme, implying that one must look forward to a succession of such programmes and a long-term IMF involvement in development finance under present arrangements. In the past it has always been assumed that Fund involvement should be occasional and episodic rather than continuing, and one may wonder whether confusion between these two roles may not prejudice the Fund's ability to act effectively in the event of a crisis.

---

[1] Some people seem to argue that the IMF should help all its members, on equity grounds. But poor countries would still get benefits in terms of policy advice, hopefully crisis avoidance and crisis resolution under the ODC proposals, as well as access under the CFF. The Fund might usefully consider the case for improving access to the CFF.

Supporters of the status quo are likely to argue that the Fund is a more effective vehicle for dispensing conditionality than is the Bank. The author has served in both organisations and can confirm that they have a valid point. There is no question but that the Fund's hierarchical organisation is more effective in producing timely and coherent action than the loose organisation and pluralism in ideas that characterise the Bank.

However, two counter-arguments deserve attention. One is that the way a bureaucracy develops is in part a consequence of what it is asked to do. Since the Bank has not in the past had any responsibility for organising a PRGF-type programme, it is not surprising that it does not have up and running the capacity to do so. The question is whether there are convincing reasons for supposing that the Bank would be incapable of developing such capacity should it be given the responsibility for the PRGF.

The other counter-argument is that the PRGF is not intended to replicate the pattern of past conditionality. On the contrary, lending under this programme is to be guided by a Poverty Reduction Strategy Paper (PRSP), which is to be prepared by the borrowing government in consultation with its civil society and private sector (as well as with the Fund and Bank). The intention is to ensure that the programme has local ownership, something that recent research has demonstrated conclusively to be of key importance if reforms are to deliver. The danger is that the PRSP will prove to be a mere fig leaf which the Fund dictates, as it has so often dictated conditionality in the past (which is also supposed to be the borrowing government's own programme). Some Fund staff members regard ownership and conditionality as antithetical – conditionality ought to require, in their view, a country to do things that it does not want to do. The logic is that conditionality is used as a device to ration access to cheap IMF credit; make the conditions the perpetuation of sensible past policies, and the IMF would soon be flooded by requests to borrow. One may have serious doubts about the ability of an organisation in which such attitudes exist to make the intellectual leap to lending on the basis of programmes that enjoy ownership. The Bank, in contrast, has worked quite hard in recent years to foster local ownership, and would therefore be much better placed to initiate a programme in which ownership is key.

Another change suggested by the ODC report concerns the collection and dissemination of statistics (p. 12). It urges that both the IMF and the World Bank should hive off their statistics operations and that these should be placed in a separate and independent agency devoted exclusively to collecting and publishing economic data. This would be a useful change, which would preclude the potential danger that a conflict of interest could corrode data, as well as centralise statistical expertise.

The discussion of surveillance above also noted the substantial measure of consensus on the Fund's role in surveillance, particularly concerning the desirability of increasing transparency. In fact the Fund has already come a long way in this direction. The author of this paper recalls his pride in being so subversive as to publish the text of a Letter of Intent in Williamson (1983). The IMF now routinely publishes the text of Letters of Intent, and much more, on its website. There is widespread consensus that the Fund could usefully focus attention on vulnerabilities stemming from weaknesses in the financial system, the level and maturity structure of foreign debt, and progress in implementing the sundry international standards currently being developed. This paper also endorses the CFR view that the Fund should actively encourage potentially vulnerable countries to impose appropriate capital inflow taxes.

There remains one major area where this paper (like the ODC report) is out of sympathy with the current conventional wisdom. This concerns the question as to whether all intermediate exchange rate regimes should be discouraged by IMF surveillance (for emerging markets and industrial countries, if not necessarily for low-income countries where capital mobility is still low) in favour of one or other of the two 'corner solutions', either a currency board or a floating rate. The author of this paper has discussed this extensively elsewhere (Williamson, 2000), but would not deny that intermediate regimes are probably more prone to crisis than the corners. The point is that they also offer benefits that the corners do not, namely the possibility of resisting the misalignments that are so often generated by both fixed and floating exchange rate regimes. If one judges that a seriously misaligned exchange rate jeopardises the possibility of rapid and sustained growth, this is serious and suggests that one should resist the temptation to focus surveillance exclusively on crisis avoidance. Important as that is, countries should also be encouraged to make the most of their growth potential.

Nevertheless, the major differences about the future of the Fund are concerned with its role as a lender rather than with surveillance. Everyone agrees that the Fund should have a central role in any financing that may occur in the context of a macro crisis, but that is about the extent of agreement. The disputed issues are:

◆   the range of facilities under which the Fund should lend;

◆   the role, if any, of pre-qualification in the Fund's lending operations;

◆   the role, if any, of a payments standstill in accompanying Fund crisis lending;

◆   the terms on which the Fund lends.

The Range of the Fund's Facilities. At present the Fund is able to lend under six different facilities: traditional standbys; the high-interest Supplementary Reserve Facility (SRF) introduced in 1998; the Contingency Credit Line (CCL) announced in 1998 but so far unutilised; the Extended Fund Facility (EFF) introduced in 1975 with the objective of allowing the Fund to make longer-term loans to developing countries experiencing a payments problem with a structural origin; the PRGF, through which the Fund makes low-interest loans to low-income members; and the Compensatory Financing Facility (CFF) which dates from the 1960s and makes low-conditionality loans to countries experiencing an exogenous and temporary shortfall in export proceeds, a surge in the cost of cereal imports or an increase in interest costs. This already represents a significant rationalisation compared with the situation prevailing before the spring 2000 meetings of the IMFC, which eliminated the Currency Stabilisation Fund, the Buffer Stock Financing Facility and support for commercial bank debt reduction (i.e. the Brady Plan). This paper has already argued that the PRGF should be transferred to the World Bank. One needs also to ask whether further streamlining would be appropriate.

To start at the end, there is a strong logical case for retaining the CFF. This is a mechanism whereby the international community helps primary-producing countries to cope with shocks that are truly exogenous with respect to their own behaviour, without requiring them to devote their own real resources to building up reserves ahead of time. It economises on the need to build up reserves.

An equally persuasive case cannot be made for retaining the EFF. When this was introduced, in the 1970s, many middle-income countries were only just establishing access to the international capital market. The World Bank did not have a capacity to lend for adjustment; its lending was all project-directed. Hence such countries could not rely on being able to borrow in order to adjust to a payments shock with a structural origin, so it seemed reasonable for the Fund to provide a facility to respond to this need. But times have changed – in three ways. One is that most middle-income countries can now borrow on the international capital market. Another is that the World Bank has since moved into structural adjustment lending, which is able to cope with very much the same type of situation. The third is that the low-income countries that are excluded from the international capital market are now accommodated by the Fund through the PRGF, which will still be available to them even if it is relocated to the World Bank. Bulgaria perhaps provides the strongest recent case for arguing that the EFF still has a role, but it is not obvious that Bulgaria could not have been accommodated through a

World Bank structural adjustment loan.

That brings us to the CCL. This was introduced with the hope that countries that felt themselves liable to be exposed to contagion would be able to fortify their liquidity to a point that would deter any speculative attack. But, as noted, no country has so far applied for a CCL, and one needs to ask why. It is not difficult to find a plausible explanation. Application is in itself liable to be interpreted by the market as an admission that the country fears a speculative attack, an interpretation that is liable to provoke the very attack that it is hoped to deter. Even if that danger is circumvented, there is a similar danger that an attack could be induced if the Fund ever found it necessary to withdraw a country's eligibility to borrow. Then there is the fact that the Fund has judged it necessary to avoid a completely automatic right-to-draw even after a country has been declared eligible, and envisages an attenuated, but nonetheless substantive, process of review that could end with the imposition of additional conditionality. Thus it is not difficult to see why the CCL has so far failed to appeal to potential candidates. It is difficult to see this lack of interest ever changing by fiddling about with interest incentives. The obvious conclusion is that it would be sensible to abolish the CCL, while absorbing some of the features of its design into the other facilities designed to allow the Fund to respond to crises.

Those other facilities are standbys and the SRF. Everyone, even the IFIAC majority, agrees that the Fund needs to be able to lend in a crisis situation. The questions are: under what conditions, on what terms, and in what quantities? While it seems quite sensible to envisage larger lending (relative to quota) carrying a higher interest rate, it is difficult to see what advantage is gained by having a separate window for the higher-interest lending. Accordingly, this paper recommends consolidating both facilities into a single window, which one might call the Crisis Facility, since its purpose is precisely to allow the Fund to help countries deal with crisis situations.[1]

Thus the Fund would be streamlined so that it offered two facilities. The CFF would provide low-conditionality loans in response to shocks that were clearly outside a country's own control, such as shortfalls in the value of primary commodity exports. It would seem logical to include also other exogenous shocks, including natural disasters (such as the 1998

---

[1]This bears some similarity to the CFR proposal to consolidate the SRF and the CCL into a new contagion facility, although the lack of conditionality envisaged for the contagion facility strikes me as unrealistic and differs significantly from my subsequent proposals.

floods in Bangladesh). The Crisis Facility would make loans in situations of macro-economic crisis.

Pre-qualification. While this paper has argued that the CCL is unattractive to potential borrowers for very basic reasons, it would be a mistake to dismiss the line of analysis that motivated its creation. The wisdom of the IFIAC majority recommendation that (after a transitional period) the Fund should lend only to countries that had pre-qualified is questionable. Nevertheless, the idea that countries should be able to borrow more, and/or more easily, and/or more cheaply is one with considerable merit if the countries have pre-satisfied certain conditions.

The attractions are most obvious with respect to the Crisis Facility. One wants to encourage countries to take actions that will minimise their vulnerability to crisis, and it seems natural to reward those that do by giving them assured access (or at least semi-assured access) to a lender of last resort (or at least to a quasi-lender of last resort). The key question is, then, what actions should be required to pre-qualify? The majority IFIAC report suggests four:

◆ freedom of entry and operation for foreign financial institutions;

◆ well-capitalised commercial banks, preferably with part of the capital in the form of uninsured subordinated debt;

◆ regular and timely publication of the maturity structure of outstanding sovereign and guaranteed debt and off-balance sheet liabilities;

◆ 'a proper fiscal requirement.'

The first of these is problematic. Traditionally countries have been allowed to decide for themselves whether or not they wish to allow entry of foreign banks. There is a legitimate economic reason why countries may, under some circumstances, hesitate to allow foreign banks to enter, namely that this can erode the franchise value of existing banks, and therefore precipitate 'gambling for redemption'. Nor does there appear to be any empirical evidence that foreign banks can be relied on to stand by a country in times of crisis by increasing their exposure; indeed, the foreign banks in Argentina froze their exposure during the 'tequila' crisis in 1995. Thus this proposal would seem at best premature.

In contrast, a requirement of a solvent, well-capitalised, and well-supervised banking system would appear entirely appropriate. The worst crises happen when a weak banking system deters a central bank from raising interest rates as needed, so that a currency crisis and a banking crisis occur simultaneously. And the suggestion that a part of bank capital should be required to take the form of uninsured subordinated debt held by third parties is also compelling; its attraction is that the holders of such debt have no possibility of upside gains from risky bank behaviour, so that they can be relied on to monitor and penalise any gambling behaviour by bank management. In asking how one might go about implementing this requirement, an attractive possibility would be to adopt the suggestion of the CFR report (and the IFIAC minority) that the test should be whether a country has adopted and implemented the Basle Core Principles. One might also ask whether it might not make sense to extend the principle to reward observance of some of the many other codes of standards currently being prepared, but, at least initially, it may be best not to overburden the system by making too many demands on surveillance.

The requirement for regular and timely publication of statistics regarding the maturity structure of sovereign debt (and off-balance sheet sovereign liabilities) is also sensible and unobjectionable. The obvious question it raises, however, is whether data on sovereign debt will suffice. None of the East Asian countries had a serious problem with sovereign debt: the problems arose with private sector debt, incurred either by banks (for example South Korea) or the corporate sector (for example Indonesia). Accumulating accurate and timely data on private sector debt raises altogether more formidable difficulties than are posed by sovereign debt. It so happens that the Fund has already established a standard on this topic, which embodies a judgment as to how much data it is reasonable to expect a country to collect. The criterion for a country to receive preferential treatment should be that it subscribes to the Fund's Special Data Dissemination Standard.

The IFIAC report does not attempt to spell out the nature of the 'proper fiscal requirement' that it suggests including as a pre-qualification requirement, presumably because this was added at the last moment in response to the objections of the minority that its absence would expose the Fund to supporting countries with runaway budget deficits. It is nonetheless not difficult to imagine the form that such a requirement might take. Perhaps it would be like the Maastricht fiscal requirement for joining the EMU: a budget deficit no greater than 3 per cent of GDP and a ratio of public sector debt to GDP of under 60 per cent (or trending down). Or perhaps it would be expressed in terms of the primary balance, to avoid the objection that a criterion expressed in terms of the total deficit could act as an inappropriate deterrent to tightening monetary policy (though this creates the problem that the necessary primary balance varies across countries depending on their level of public sector debt). Or perhaps it would be expressed in terms of the cyclically-adjusted balance, to avoid the objection that a criterion expressed in terms of the crude deficit could act as an inappropriate deterrent to an anti-cyclical fiscal policy. Or perhaps it should be expressed in terms of the operational deficit, to avoid making unreasonable demands on countries that have still not eliminated a high inertial inflation. Or perhaps it would be better not to try to lay down a universal requirement to be met by all countries, but instead to have the Fund make a regular judgment on a country's fiscal position.

That, then, raises the question as to why the Fund's judgment should be restricted to the fiscal dimension. Why not have the Fund's Article IV consultation end with the award of a rating of the country's overall macro-economic policy? One would surely want this rating to be more like those of the ratings agencies than the simple yes/no rating embodied in the CCL, so that countries can be downgraded when they deserve it without automatically provoking Armageddon in the markets. Having such a rating awarded regularly by an official institution would also resolve the problem of what to use to determine the risk ratings used in calculating bank capital adequacy requirements.

One other idea merits inclusion, in addition to the conditions suggested by the IFIAC report. This is the suggestion in the Geneva report (p. 71) that the IMF should provide an incentive by lending on more attractive terms to countries that include appropriate provisions in bond covenants to make their bonds renegotiable under crisis conditions. These provisions 'would include majority representation, sharing, non-acceleration, minimum legal action threshold and collective representation clauses, where these last provisions allow an indenture trustee to represent and co-ordinate the bondholders'.

Hence the suggestions of a list of pre-qualification criteria that would entitle countries to draw from the Fund under the crisis facility on enhanced terms:

◆ adoption and implementation of the Basle Core Principles for the domestic banking system;

◆ subscription to the Special Data Dissemination Standard;

◆ a good rating for macro-economic policy in the most recent Article IV consultation, and inclusion of collective action and allied clauses in its foreign bonds, especially sovereign bonds.

How about drawings from the other facility that this paper has argued the Fund should retain – the CFF? Many of the countries that are most likely to suffer strong variations in commodity prices are unlikely to have banking systems that have advanced to the point of implementing all the Basle Core Principles. Similarly, they may not be able to afford a statistical service sufficiently sophisticated to be capable of subscribing to the SDDS. It would be unfair to penalise them for not meeting the full standards expected for crisis borrowers. They should, nonetheless, face the same requirement of good macro-economic policy as any other borrower, and they might also be rewarded for any of the other conditions that they meet.

Payments Standstills. Three of the six sources analysed in this paper – the Geneva report, the CFR report and Secretary Summers's speech – saw a role for standstills in dealing with at least some capital account crises. (The subject is not taken up in the other three reports.) All of them regard standstills as something to be deployed as a last resort rather than embodied as a regular element of crisis management.

This is a topic on which the conventional wisdom is deeply unrealistic. The world tried for many years after 1945 to deny that sovereign debts ever needed to be restructured, but the Brady Plan finally acknowledged that this is not tenable. Not all contingencies are foreseeable, and hence, no matter how conscientious the debtor, contingencies may arise in which it is something between unreasonably costly and totally impossible for the debtor to maintain debt service according to the original contractual terms. This is now widely acknowledged, but its corollary is not. That corollary is that any creditor that suspects restructuring to be a possibility has an incentive to liquidate its claim while that remains possible. Limited official loans will simply allow more creditors to get out, rather than encourage them to stay in. The choice is between unlimited official loans (a real lender of last resort rather than a quasi-lender of last resort) and restructuring the debt. In any single instance the provision of unlimited liquidity may well be the most attractive option, provided at least that the country really has got its fundamentals in order so that its problem is indeed one of illiquidity rather than insolvency. But, even if one is not sure that past IMF loans have been a major source of moral hazard in the way the IFIAC majority believe, it seems quite implausible that promulgation of such a policy would not create moral hazard in the future. If one worries about that, the logical conclusion is that the IMF should never undertake crisis lending except in the context of a standstill. An essential component of the policies needed to deal with a capital account crisis has to be reconstruction of debt on terms that the country can respect, and until that has been accomplished it is foolhardy to try to maintain debt service.

This means that a country that decided it needed to borrow from the Fund would be expected to declare a standstill while it negotiated with the Fund. It would start negotiating with at least some of its private creditors at the same time, with an overwhelming presumption that problems of illiquidity should be handled by extending maturities rather than reducing the present value of debt-service obligations. The IMF might provide bridging loans while the negotiations were in progress, provided it was convinced that the country was negotiating with its creditors in good faith. It would conclude the negotiations only when it was convinced that the restructured debt profile agreed between debtor and creditors was one that the country could be expected to service according to the new contractual terms. At that point the country would also lift its standstill and start servicing its debt on the revised terms. Note that these arrangements give an incentive to both parties to seek a prompt debt restructuring: the debtor will be denied bridge financing from the Fund if it does not negotiate in good faith, and the creditors will not see debt service resumed until the negotiations have been completed.

This paper goes along with the bulk of the literature in assuming that it would be the country, rather than the IMF, that would declare a standstill. It would presumably do this at the same time that it announced that it was approaching the Fund. The difficulties in declaring a standstill are not as great as is frequently asserted. It is arguable that there is no need for a set of well-defined rules regarding coverage. The country would have a strong incentive to make coverage as broad as is necessary to re-establish its financial standing, since it would know that no IMF loan would be forthcoming unless enough of its debt was restructured to allow it to service its debt. If that could be achieved by restructuring only sovereign debt, and without an element of discrimination unacceptable to the Paris Club, then presumably the country would choose to limit the standstill to sovereign debt. But if it knew that the Paris Club would demand parallel treatment for London Club debt, it would be foolhardy not to extend the standstill immediately to bank debt as well, since every bank would have an overwhelming incentive to liquidate whatever loans it could before the standstill that, in that circumstance, it would have to expect would go into effect. The same applies to bonds if the Paris Club demanded similar treatment of bonds. And if it is unlikely that the country could get back on its feet without restructuring corporate debt, or while capital flight is in progress, then it would also be well-advised to impose exchange controls that would suspend the servicing of corporate debt and/or control capital flight. But there is no need for the IMF to lay down rules about the extent of the standstill that it would expect to accompany an approach for money. The country could be left to choose how extensive to make the standstill.

Critics of the standstill idea usually worry about the impact that legalisation of standstills might have on the flow of credit to borrowing countries. Would lenders not be so worried about the possibility of a standstill being imposed as to decline to lend significant sums? One could indeed imagine that reaction if a borrower had a unilateral right to impose a standstill without any international restraint. But the version outlined above requires the Fund to certify that the debtor is negotiating to restructure its debts in good faith as a condition for receiving interim finance, and that it gets a final agreement only after the debts have been successfully restructured. This should usually accelerate a country's return to health, including servicing debt on contractual terms. A creditor who knew that any currently unforeseeable debt problems would be handled in this expeditious way should be a more, not less, attractive client. It is only when a country had built up its debts to a point where a crisis began to be feared that its creditors would have a good reason for not lending; but it is in those circumstances that many of us feel it to be highly desirable for lenders to show more restraint. It is probably true that a standstill requirement would bring crises forward in time, and might even prevent the occasional case of a country with a potential crisis that manages to fight it off by prompt action, but even this would have a countervailing advantage in that it would be altogether more likely that countries would be brought to restructure their debts before a write-down was necessary. As creditors came to accept that the norm would be an extension of maturities, rather than a loss of present value, so any deterrent effect (other than in circumstances when debt was already excessive) would vanish.

Loan Terms. This concerns the questions of how large a loan countries should be entitled to, of the maturity of those loans, and of the interest rates they should be required to pay.

Some of the assertions that IMF loans could be reduced in size seem to be based more on faith than analysis. This paper has already argued that one would need indefinitely large loans in order to ensure the restoration of market confidence without an accompanying private sector debt restructuring. The addition of the requirement of a standstill and a private debt restructuring is essential if one wishes to limit the size of IMF loans and still be confident that they could restore a country's financial standing.

The IFIAC report suggests limiting IMF loans to 120 days, with the possibility of only one rollover. The reason it gives for this recommendation is that: '[h]istorical experience suggests that liquidity crises typically last for a matter of weeks or, in extreme cases, for several months' (p. 46). This is naïve – the reason liquidity crises are short-lived is that private lenders are soon able to see where the country is going to be able to get the resources to service its debts. A sure-fire way of lengthening crises would be to make the Fund's credits sufficiently short term to keep private lenders guessing as to whether the country would be capable of honouring its debt-service obligations when the Fund has to be repaid. The maturity of the Fund's existing standby facility, namely 3–5 years, seems altogether more appropriate.

The IFIAC report suggested that Fund lending should be done at a penalty interest rate (defined as 'a premium over the sovereign yield paid by the member country one week prior to applying for an IMF loan', p. 46). This runs counter to the tradition by which the Fund lent on the finest terms that any sovereign could command, a tradition inspired by the idea of an international self-help co-operative. The disadvantage of this tradition is that it can tempt a rational government into regarding the Fund as a preferred source of credit, deterring prompt repayment of loans and conceivably even tempting it into qualifying for new loans (although this would normally require staging a crisis, which governments do not usually find attractive). A solution suggested in the ODC report is that the interest rate should be progressively increased as the duration of a Fund loan increases, thus providing an incentive for prompt repayment without threatening the effectiveness of a loan in the way that a short maturity would.

The ODC report argues that a concessional interest rate would be needed for low-income countries if their theoretical right to draw were to be a reality. This also seems a compelling argument, and not necessarily in conflict with the idea of a rate that becomes progressively more penal as time proceeds. The rate for these countries could start at a highly concessional level and then increase progressively over time.

The final idea that ought to be integrated into the interest rate structure is that countries should be given an incentive to take steps that would minimise the chance of their needing to borrow from the Fund. That is, countries would face a lower interest rate the more fully they satisfied the conditions listed above.

The result of taking all three of these factors into account in determining the interest rate to be charged for a loan from the Fund would be to produce a complex interest rate schedule rather than the simple pattern of either rate A or rate B. This is no great disaster. Computers are very good at doing the arithmetic that would be necessary to keep track of payments due. It would also have the great advantage of increasing the penalties paid by countries for policy slippage in marginal instalments, rather than confronting the Fund with the awful prospect of precipitating a certain crisis if it recognised worsening performance.

Concluding Remarks

There have been many calls in recent months for the Fund to get back to basics or to focus on its areas of core competence, which everyone agrees lie in macro policy, crisis avoidance and crisis management. The reform programme laid out in the preceding section of this paper is intended to do that, and to do it without emasculating the Fund in the way that the IFIAC majority would. It would not only return the Fund to the areas of its core competence, but it would strip the Fund down to two lending facilities, one designed to allow countries to replenish their liquidity when faced by exogenous shocks, and the other to help countries respond to crisis situations. It recognises that in a world of high capital mobility this is almost bound to involve debt restructuring, and therefore calls for countries applying for an IMF loan to impose a standstill on debt-service payments, an approach that would deal once and for all with the danger of creditor moral hazard. It suggests the use of variable interest rates on loans to build an appropriate pattern of incentives for member countries to choose policies that would minimise the danger of their encountering a crisis, and that would enable and encourage them to repay the Fund promptly when they found it necessary to borrow. While it returns the Fund to its areas of core competence, these are ones that are of major importance to even the poorest members of the Fund, ensuring that the IMF would continue to play a vital role in the world economy.

References

Askari, Hossein and Samir Chebil (1999). 'Reforming the IMF: Some organizational and operational issues', *Banca Nazionale del Lavoro Quarterly Review*.

Ahluwalia, Montek (1999). 'The IMF and the World Bank in the New Financial Architecture', in *International Monetary and Financial Issues for the 1990s*, vol. XI. New York and Geneva: United Nations. Referred to as 'the Ahluwalia report'.

Council on Foreign Relations Independent Task Force (1999). *Safeguarding Prosperity in a Global Financial System: The Future International Financial Architecture*. Washington: Institute for International Economics. Referred to as 'the CFR report'.

De Gregorio, Jose, Barry Eichengreen, Takatoshi Ito and Charles Wyplosz (undated but apparently 1999). *An Independent and Accountable IMF*. Geneva: International Centre for Monetary and Banking Studies and London: Centre for Economic Policy Research. Referred to as the 'Geneva report'.

International Financial Institution Advisory Commission (2000). *Report of the International Financial Institution Advisory Commission*. Washington: no publisher specified. Referred to as 'the IFIAC report'.

Krugman, Paul (2000). 'Errors of Commission', *New York Times*, 8 March.

Overseas Development Council (2000). *The Future Role of the IMF in Development*. Washington: ODC. Referred to as 'the ODC report'.

Summers, Lawrence (1999). 'The Right Kind of IMF for a Stable Global Financial System'. Speech at the London Business School, December 14.

Williamson, John (1983). *IMF Conditionality*. Washington: Institute for International Economics.

Williamson, John (2000). *Exchange Rate Regimes for Emerging Markets: Reviving the Intermediate Option*. Washington: Institute for International Economics.

Future Role of the IMF:
A Developing Country Point of View

Aziz Ali Mohammed

Introduction

This paper seeks to address some of the issues that have arisen from the recent world-wide debates on the future role of the International Monetary Fund in the wake of its management of the Mexican, Asian, Russian and Brazilian financial crises. The debates have been particularly intense in the USA during and since the passage of legislation in the US Congress for the authorisation of an increase in the US quota and its credit line in the New Arrangements to Borrow (NAB), and following the submission of a report by a US Congressional Commission headed by Professor Alan Meltzer.[1]

At one extreme is a position taken by conservatives like former US Treasury Secretary George Schultz who proposes the abolition of the IMF on the grounds that its crisis lending operations generate an unacceptable degree of moral hazard for the private financial system, as well as for sovereign borrowers. In the same camp are abolitionists on the far left of the political spectrum who regard the IMF as the modern-day replacement of 18th-century 'gun-boat' diplomacy. They are convinced that the IMF serves the imperialist designs of its principal shareholders, and imposes harsh conditionalities on the populations of poor countries to ensure the servicing of debts owed to creditor governments and financial institutions in the advanced capitalist countries. Others with a less hostile orientation advocate the merging of the IMF into the World Bank Group.

At the other extreme is the view that if the IMF did not exist, it would have to be invented. It is regarded by its supporters as playing a constructive role as an international credit co-operative serving its universal membership with impartial macro-economic policy advice, technical assistance and financing for countries encountering temporary balance of payments problems. At this end of the spectrum, the debate focuses on how to enlarge its role in the global economy in a variety of ways: as a genuine lender of last resort and as creator of international liquidity through its prototype SDR mechanism; as an umpire in orderly debt negotiations between creditors, private and official, and their sovereign

[1]International Financial Institution Advisory Commission (IFIAC) Report, 8 March 2000.

125

debtors; as an international authority endowed with powers to declare a 'standstill' on legal actions that private creditors might take to enforce their claims on sovereign debtors; and, finally, as an overseer of the international monetary system, exercising effective surveillance over the exchange rate policies of the major international currency countries.

Within this broad range of views, a series of intermediate positions have been advanced by official and non-official groups, including academics and representatives of non-governmental organisations and by representatives of developing countries.[1] The majority in the Meltzer Commission would restrict the IMF to a crisis prevention and response role through very short-term, essentially unconditional, liquidity support for a limited number of relatively strong emerging countries which have pre-qualified for IMF assistance. The main report would eliminate the Poverty Reduction and Growth Facility (PRGF), restrict IMF surveillance to non-OECD member countries and write off all IMF claims against its Heavily Indebted Poor Country (HIPC) members. However, four members of the Meltzer Commission have taken a sharply different view on some of the major recommendations made by the Commission's majority report.[2] In an address in London[3] delivered late last year, US Treasury Secretary Lawrence Summers observed: 'to say that the IMF is indispensable is not to say that we can be satisfied with the one we now have'. He then proceeded to argue that in a world dominated by private capital flows, the IMF must accept 'a more selective role that is focused on emergency situations' and 'a more limited role in the poorest countries focused on growth and poverty reduction'. The PRGF would be maintained and selectivity in respect of other transactions would be enforced by lending for shorter maturities and at higher interest charges.

---

[1] The US Treasury, responding to the IFIAC Report in a document dated 8 June 2000, finds itself 'in fundamental disagreement' with that Report's core recommendations for further reform. Among recent non-official reports from US bodies, mention may be made of three: (1) Council on Foreign Relations Independent Task Force (CFR) *Report on the Future of the International Financial Architecture*, New York, September 1999; (2) International Center for Monetary and Banking Studies, Geneva and Center for Economic Policy Research, London *Report on An Independent and Accountable IMF*, 1999; and (3) Overseas Development Council (ODC) Report *The Future Role of the IMF in Development*, Washington DC, April 2000. An unofficial G-24 position is articulated in a paper prepared by Montek Ahluwalia titled 'The IMF and the World Bank in the New Financial Architecture' in *International Monetary and Financial Issues for the 1990s*, Vol XI, New York and Geneva, United Nations, 1999; official G-24 positions are stated in the press communiques of the Group issued in September 1999 and April 2000 (reproduced in the IMF *Survey*).

[2] Joint Dissenting Statement signed by four members: C. Fred Bergsten, Richard Huber, Jerome Levinson and Esteban Edward Torres; three of them did not sign the main Report.

[3] 'The Right Kind of IMF for a Stable Global System', delivered at the London Business School on 14 December 1999.

The US Treasury response broadly follows the lines of the Treasury Secretary's London address.

In another recent report from official sources,[1] the UK Treasury Committee is not convinced that 'the IMF has the correct expertise to undertake major debt relief programmes in developing countries'. It wants the IMF to 'pull back from such programmes and concentrate on its original mandate'. It warns that unless the roles of the IMF and the World Bank Group are clarified: 'the level of overlap increases the argument for a merger'. The Committee urges that a major area of the Fund's work – on codes, international standards and financial regulation – should be given a 'higher priority'.

The positions articulated in the preceding paragraphs by authoritative sources in some of the principal shareholder members of the Fund stand in contrast to several major addresses delivered by the former Managing Director of the IMF, Michel Camdessus, in the days just prior to his retirement[2] and to the submission made by Stanley Fischer, First Deputy Managing Director, to the Meltzer Commission.[3] The new Managing Director of the IMF, Horst Köhler, has also now begun to articulate his preliminary thinking on the role of the Fund.[4]

In the following sections, the main issues regarding the Fund's role are discussed, using the arguments of the protagonists but without identifying the source of each argument. Rather the objective is to present both sides of the issue as a backdrop to articulating a developing country position.

Issues Arising from Recent Policy Declarations and Reports

Several issues have been the subject of contention in recent days. It is proposed to review them in the following paragraphs. Some of the argumentation is inevitably repetitive since the issues are overlapping.

Country eligibility for IMF assistance: As noted earlier, a strong case has been made for restricting the Fund's financing role to emerging market

---

[1] HM Treasury, Third Report, Treasury Committee, Session 1999–2000.

[2] Remarks at the Council on Foreign Relations entitled 'An agenda for the IMF at the start of the 21st Century' (New York) and at the Institute for the Study of Diplomacy, School of Foreign Service, Georgetown University, entitled 'The IMF We Need', both in February 2000.

[3] Presentation to the IFIAC on 2 February 2 2000.

[4] Notably in a speech delivered to the International Monetary Conference in Paris, 30 May 2000. IMF *Survey*, Vol. 29, No 11, 5 June 2000.

economies in financial crises and to providing them with short-term emergency loans at penalty interest rates. The basic argument for restricting the IMF role to that of a quasi-lender of last resort in a limited number of cases is that Fund operations generate moral hazard for both private lenders and sovereign borrowers. The Fund's intervention is said to allow short-term creditors (such as the international banks whose claims are not 'marked to market') to be paid off in full and, in the case of other creditors, its action is said to delay mutually negotiated debt work-outs. Moreover, interruptions in Fund programmes due to the difficulty of meeting the number and variety of conditions attaching to IMF programmes are said to impair the return of confidence in the borrowing country. Finally, the austerity prescriptions incorporated in Fund programmes are said to impose enormous costs on both debtor governments and the general population, especially wage-earners. Much is made of the 'ambiguous' evidence of the impact of Fund programmes in many countries and their usefulness is said to be confined only to cases where financial crises in 'systemically significant' countries can produce, through contagion, serious consequences for otherwise solvent trading and investment partners.

The fundamental flaw in arguing from the evidence of past IMF programmes is that it fails to consider the counterfactual. The 'before' and 'after' dichotomy leaves no room for 'with' and 'without' considerations, i.e. what would have transpired if the Fund had not intervened. The argument for restricting Fund action to countries that are 'systemically significant' assumes that these can be unequivocally identified in advance. As Michel Camdessus asks: 'who prior to July 1997 would have regarded Thailand as belonging to the "systemically significant" category?'

The growing integration of an increasing number of developing countries into global financial markets has created a powerful case for treating member countries of the IMF on a more, rather than a less, equal basis when it comes to access to IMF financial support. Also not to be ignored are the legal rights and obligations of members as laid down in the Fund's Articles of Agreement and the accumulated precedents and practices of the Fund as they have evolved over the past 50 years. These create a powerful equity case for universal access to the resources of a credit co-operative to which all members have contributed.

Involvement in poverty alleviation and debt reduction (HIPC) cases: The principal argument for pulling the IMF out of the poverty alleviation area is that as a short-term balance of payments adjustment lender, its core competency is, and should remain, macro-economic policy analysis. The

IMF is said to lack the wide expertise required to deal with poverty issues,[1] which have deep-rooted structural and institutional causes, and which are only treatable over the very long term. There is also the argument that if the IMF were to try to build its expertise in the poverty area, this would add to the degree of overlap that already prevails vis-à-vis the World Bank Group and that this would strengthen the argument for merging the two institutions. Finally, there is a strongly held view on the part of some in the NGO community that by clothing it with the mantle of poverty – by changing the name of the Enhanced Structural Adjustment Facility to the Poverty Reduction and Growth Facility G-7 – governments are seeking to maintain the IMF's traditional role as gate-keeper for debt relief operations, and thereby to justify the application of IMF conditionality to even the poorest of its member countries.

There are several counter-arguments to the preceding view. Poverty alleviation is simply not possible without a strong macro-economic policy environment and the IMF has a unique expertise in designing the essential policy requirements in this crucial sphere. But advice is not likely to be taken seriously unless there is a promise of financial help to go with it. This is not a matter of 'bribing' decision-makers to undertake reform. Rather, it is only realistic to recognise that countries are not monolithic entities and the pressures exerted by the spending ministries (like the military) within the government for larger budgets are difficult for policy-makers concerned with financial sustainability to resist unless they can deploy some countervailing arguments in support of their belt-tightening recommendations. Indeed, there are always interest groups outside government that are beneficiaries of the status quo (for example, employers who would rather hire child labour instead of paying adult wages) and who are apt to be well-represented within the governing elites. Reformers within governments must be able to point to some visible, palpable benefit from pursuing pro-poor policies and this means that the IMF must have resources to offer to back up good advice and technical assistance. Moreover, as pointed out by Stanley Fischer: 'governments and markets alike appear to place greater value on financial agreements with the Fund, possibly because the provision of resources is still seen to represent a greater commitment by the official sector'.[2]

---

[1] As an example, Paul Collier and Jan Willem Gunning argue that 'both the sectoral and the household-level analyses needed for a reasonable estimation of the social consequences of adjustment . . . are beyond the Fund's traditional expertise . . . . Fund staff have been recruited for their expertise in macro-economics.' *Economic Journal* 109. Royal Economic Society, November 1999, F634–F651.

[2] Op.cit., fn 7, supra.

Moreover, the IMF has a long record of working with the poorer countries in its membership who are just as likely as better-off countries to suffer balance of payments difficulties from a variety of causes, including terms of trade shocks, crop failures, export market disruptions and natural disasters, not to speak of bad economic management. The international community has recognised that poor countries will need IMF help but cannot afford to pay regular Fund charges. It has therefore been willing to entrust the IMF with the necessary means to subsidise its dealings with these members rather than depriving them of the right of access enjoyed by all members under the Articles of Agreement.

The launching of the HIPC in 1996, and its enhancement in 1999, has reinforced the need for the role which the IMF has traditionally played in the Paris Club, and in its handling of the Latin American debt problems of the 1980s and of the problems of transitional countries in the 1990s. Creditor countries want debt relief offered under the HIPC to be used to increase spending on poverty alleviation; they also want an assurance that the debtor country will follow prudent macro-economic policies so that a debt problem will not recur. They have been prepared to allow the IMF to mobilise a part of its 'hidden' reserve (in the shape of gold holdings that are carried on its books at far below the current market price) in order to enable the IMF to provide relief on its own claims against countries eligible for debt relief under the HIPC programme. The IMF has also been able to mobilise additional bilateral funding from as many as 93 of its members (which indicates that a large number of developing country members have contributed) to the PRGF-HIPC Trust for an amount which exceeded $1.5 billion by the end of April 2000. There is no assurance that a large part of the commitments obtained by the IMF will not simply fall away because donor governments will be unwilling to go back to their legislative bodies to authorise the switching of appropriations to the World Bank if the PRGF is transferred to that institution. Indeed there is a strong risk that this might happen.

Nor should IMF involvement necessarily require that it develops its own intensive expertise in all aspects of poverty alleviation. The IMF management has recognised the need for close co-ordination and a clear delineation of responsibilities between the IMF and the World Bank. Stanley Fischer, the IMF's First Deputy Managing Director, in his presentation to the Meltzer Commission, has gone on record to the effect that 'the World Bank *will take the lead* in helping countries formulate their poverty reduction strategies *and in lending for those purposes*. For its part, the IMF has to take into account the fiscal implications of anti-poverty programmes when designing the macro-economic framework. Together with the World Bank, it needs to ensure that the impact of the necessary macro-economic measures on the poor has been properly analysed and the potential adverse effects minimised – *the latter typically by means of World Bank supported programmes*[1] (emphasis supplied). Similar views are attributed to the new Managing Director. Moreover, as argued elsewhere,[2] the deadline-driven country focus of the IMF work environment provides an essential complement to the undoubted expertise that the World Bank and the other regional development banks deploy in the poverty reduction area; developing countries will want the IMF to be involved to help ensure timely outcomes in the poverty reduction and HIPC areas.

The IMF as lender of last resort (LLR): There is a general acceptance of the proposition that the IMF is the 'closest that the international financial system has to a lender of last resort';[3] but there is an unwillingness 'to confirm the IMF in this role' or to accept the logical implications of its playing this role in an effective manner. These implications were spelt out in two papers prepared for the G-24 Research Programme in September 1999;[4] they received support in one of Michel Camdessus's pre-retirement speeches in which he proposed that 'in the event of a systemic credit crunch' the IMF be 'authorised to inject additional liquidity – and to withdraw it when the need has passed – in a manner analogous to that of a national central bank, through the creation and selective allocation of SDRs'.[5] The Independent Task Force of the Council on Foreign Relations proposed a 'contagion facility [that] would be funded by pooling a one-off allocation of SDRs'.[6]

These proposals have met with strong objections from those preoccupied with the moral hazard problem. Even those who support them have contemplated invoking such a facility in 'rare situations of widespread cross-border contagion of financial crises where failure to intervene would

---

[1]The US Treasury Response takes a similar line when arguing that there has to be 'a clear division of labour between the World Bank and the IMF, with the Bank taking the lead in providing advice on the design of growth-enhancing national poverty reduction strategies and structural reforms while the Fund will focus on promoting sound macro-economic policy and structural reforms in related areas, such as tax policy and fiscal management'. Op. cit., fn 2, supra, pp. 22–23.

[2]In a paper on the 'Future Role of the World Bank Group' prepared by Aziz Ali Mohammed for the Commonwealth Secretariat seminar, 22–23 June 2000. Mimeo.

[3]Op. cit., fn 6, supra.

[4]Montek S. Ahluwalia. 'The IMF and the World Bank in the New Financial Architecture'; Aziz Ali Mohammed. 'Adequacy of International Liquidity in the Current Financial Environment', in *International Monetary and Financial Issues for the 1990s*, Vol. XI. United Nations, 1999.

[5]Op. cit., fn 6, supra.

[6]Op. cit., fn 5, supra.

threaten the performance of the world economy'.[1] However, it is essential to have in place a simple mechanism which could decisively underpin confidence in the international system. The need for some such mechanism has clearly intensified in light of the continued volatility of private capital flows, the powerful resistance of private sector interests to official proposals for their involvement in the management of financial crises and the rather limited use made of the Supplemental Reserve Facility (SRF) and the non-use of Contingent Credit Lines (CCL). Hence there remains a need to continue to explore the merits of establishing an international lender of last resort. Current discussions of the pre-qualification criteria for access to a revised CCL need to proceed in tandem with an analysis of the requirements for an effective LLR, i.e. one able to create international liquidity freely and to deploy it rapidly to deal with widespread financial crises.

The IMF role in debt negotiations: In the absence of an LLR facility, the IMF has been required to provide large multiples of the quota to crisis-affected countries, as well as to call on the Multilateral Development Banks (MDBs) and individual governments for support. Apart from the problems encountered in obtaining funding, these operations are said to have generated unacceptable moral hazard for the private financial system. The solution to both these problems has been sought in options for involving the private sector in the resolution of financial crises. Little progress is noticeable because of wide differences of approach among the major financial authorities and the powerful resistance of the private financial services industry, except in the area of encouraging the use of collective action clauses in international bond contracts. From a developing country point of view, the issue needs to be framed in the broader context of evolving a more *orderly*, as well as a more *equitable*, set of arrangements to deal with the problems of sovereign debtors, so as to create an appropriate sharing of costs and responsibilities between them and their creditors, whether private or official.

In the absence of an international bankruptcy code, the existing patchwork makes for long delays in reaching agreements, during which considerable, if not irretrievable, damage is incurred by the debtor country. A first step in achieving an orderly debt work-out and 'the key to stopping an international financial panic', is 'a temporary standstill on international debt payments, much like the payments standstill that features prominently in most domestic bankruptcy proceedings'.[2] While voluntary

---

[1] Ibid.
[2] Steven Radelet. 'Orderly Workouts for Cross-Border Private Debt', Vol. XI, op.cit., fn 12 i. supra.

market-based standstills are much to be preferred, a mandatory stay on legal action by creditors has been proposed in order to minimise the risk of disruptive litigation by means of a modification or a re-interpretation of Article VIII, Section 2(b) of the IMF Articles. The chances of such options being implemented are minimal and it would be fruitless to argue for any standstill to be authorised by the IMF. Much better would be some mechanism for the debtor country itself to declare a temporary standstill, and to choose how extensive to make the standstill, while it is negotiating with the IMF for financial support.[1]

Another option for an orderly debt work-out would be the arranging of debt rollovers, as illustrated by the recent Korean case, and the possibility of providing 'financing-in-place', as is the case when the IMF is prepared to 'lend into payments arrears'. The criteria for such lending must be carefully defined; thus, the IMF must assure itself that the debtor country is negotiating in good faith with its creditors at the same time as it ensures that recalcitrant creditors do not hold up the provision of IMF assistance.

It is the framework for such negotiations that constitutes the final step in the debt work-out process. The role of the IMF in this process is a delicate one, especially if it is a creditor of the debtor country and enjoys a 'preferred creditor' status. Even otherwise, it is important to preserve the principle that the IMF is not a party to the negotiations between the country and its creditors. 'The IMF should play the role of facilitator – and not an arbiter – for an agreement between countries . . . and [their] private commercial creditors.'[2]

Surveillance issues: A number of issues are in contention in this area. One of the more easily resolved is whether IMF surveillance should be exercised on a selective basis (as proposed, for instance, by the Meltzer Commission, which would exempt OECD members) or be universal. Given the cardinal importance of the principle of the uniformity of treatment of members enshrined in the Fund's Articles of Agreement, such an opting-out provision would not be acceptable on equity grounds alone.

Another question relates to the content of surveillance, for example whether it should be restricted to the core competence of the IMF – macro-economic policy and management. There has been a widespread

---

[1] John Williamson has proposed that the IMF 'certify that the debtor is negotiating to restructure its debts in good faith as a condition for receiving interim finance, and that it gets a final agreement only after the debts have been successfully restructured'. Paper commissioned by the Commonwealth Secretariat, 'The Role of the IMF: A Guide to the Reports', May 2000. Mimeo.

[2] Speech of the President of the Central Reserve Bank of Peru, Dr. German Suarez, inaugurating the 12th Technical Group Meeting of the G-24. Lima, March 2000.

feeling among IMF critics that 'mission creep' on the part of the IMF has tended to enlarge the coverage of the surveillance exercise to the detriment of its operational focus, and that the IMF has moved into areas where it has no particular comparative advantage. On the other hand, it has been argued that 'effective, credible policy implementation hinges on the broader issues of sound economic institutions, structural reforms and the implementation of international standards'.[1] A practical argument for extending the scope of surveillance, and one which appeals to developing countries, is that because the obligation to accept the Fund's oversight applies to the entire membership, it is the only international institution that has the credibility within the financial community to serve as the lead agency for monitoring diverse areas of activity in both developed and developing countries.

Yet another issue in the surveillance area is its primary purpose. Should it be the primary means of transferring 'cutting-edge' knowledge of best practices, including the application of international standards of transparency and codes of good fiscal and monetary policies and procedures? Or should it be the main instrument of crisis prevention? While there need be no hard-and-fast choices here, there is a question to which the answer depends on who is the addressee for this function. In recent times, much emphasis has been placed on responsibility for crisis prevention and critics have argued that IMF surveillance either failed to detect the vulnerabilities in particular countries or failed to provide early warning on their likely onset. A great deal of emphasis on transparency and disclosure has been justified on the grounds that the focus of surveillance should shift from 'collecting and sharing information within the club of nations . . . to promoting the collection and dissemination of information for markets and investors.'[2] The issue goes to the *raison d'être* of a public intergovernmental institution. Whom does the IMF serve – its member governments or the private financial services industry which is mainly located in a few industrial countries? As a co-operative of governments, the IMF cannot be expected to issue public warnings that are likely to become self-fulfilling prophecies. Nor should insistence on IMF transparency be pushed to the point where it begins to affect the trust of governments in the confidentiality of their exchanges with the institution in the course of exercising the surveillance function. While the dissemination of information to markets can be justified, developing countries tend to resist pushing the IMF into the role of a super-rating agency for the benefit of private market participants.

---

[1] ODC Report, op. cit., fn 2, supra.

[2] Op. cit., fn 4, Summers.

IMF conditionality: This issue has always been a contentious one and acrimony over it intensified after IMF interventions in the East Asian countries[1] and the subsequent crises in Russia and Brazil. The main charge made by the critics is that by insisting on fiscal austerity, high interest rates and exchange rate depreciations in East Asia, and by initially supporting fixed exchange rates in Russia and Brazil and then changing course, the IMF prescriptions made a bad situation much worse. There is no question that operating in an environment of unparalleled crisis and with data either incomplete or inaccurate, the IMF staff were forced to take major decisions under enormous time and data constraints. That mistakes were made is true; the IMF did reverse course, but a good deal of damage would have been done in the interregnum. This is a risk that all policy-makers face, whether in the private or public sector, when decisions have to be made in an atmosphere of crisis and with profound uncertainties about the outcome.[2] With the V-shaped recovery under way in most of the Asian countries and in Brazil, the criticism has abated somewhat.

A quite different approach has gained some currency. The Meltzer Commission, for instance, has argued that the IMF be precluded from conditioning its support to member countries on the achievement of economic reforms, other than reforms required to meet pre-qualification conditions. Even the Commission, however, would require the IMF to establish 'a proper fiscal requirement to assure that IMF resources would not be used to sustain irresponsible budget policies'. As this paper has argued, there are always contending factions within governments and IMF conditions, including 'prior conditions', are frequently used by those advocating reform policies as a means of overcoming resistance from other parts of the official apparatus. Developing country representatives on the IMF Executive Board have, by and large, accepted IMF conditionality as a fact of life, although there has been much resistance to some of the newer conditions that have been applied under the rubric of 'governance conditionality'.[3]

---

[1] The most acrid critique was launched by Joseph Stiglitz, former World Bank Chief Economist, in an article in *New Republic*, 17 April 17 2000.

[2] Robert Rubin, a former US Treasury Secretary, has pointed out that in public life, 'critics . . . always punish risk-taking if it is unsuccessful – no matter how sound the decision may have been – and that all too often deters sensible risk taking in the public sector. . . . Too often, public servants are held to a standard of being error-free – a standard that those that suffer from the frailty of being human beings can only meet by doing nothing'. Remarks made at the World Affairs Institute Award Dinner, Washington DC, 26 April 2000.

[3] For a good analysis of this subject, see Devesh Kapur and Richard Webb. 'Governance-Related Conditionalities of the IFIs'. Paper presented at the XII Technical Group Meeting of the Intergovernmental Group of 24. Lima, Peru, March 2000. Mimeo.

Capital liberalisation: This issue has tended to recede somewhat from the peak of interest in it reached at the annual meetings of the institution in Hong Kong in 1997 when recommendations were made for investing the IMF with statutory authority to promote capital liberalisation. A number of studies conducted subsequently, both inside and outside the IMF, have adopted a position that is far less ideological; support for open capital accounts has been qualified with references to liberalisation being gradual, prudent and orderly. Developing countries would prefer a Fund position where the possibility of maintaining capital controls as a regular instrument of national policy is recognised, rather than their being regarded merely as a temporary device to deal with emergency situations in countries with poor financial regulation. This is particularly necessary to deal with the issue of the choice of exchange regimes in a world of freer capital movements. Developing countries are being pushed to choose between 'corner' solutions. They might prefer intermediate regimes supported by capital controls, whether of a market-oriented character (as in Chile in the past) or of an administrative nature.

The World Bank in a 'Globalising' World

Shahid Javed Burki[1]

For almost a decade there has been pressure on both the World Bank and the community of nations that support the institution to change in a significant way the structure and mission of the Bank. It is argued that the World Bank has outgrown its original mandate of (a) becoming an intermediary between a capital-starved developing world and international financial markets, and (b) providing technical assistance, management and finance for implementing large infrastructure projects without which – according to thinking on development at the time the Bank was established – economic growth would not occur.

There is no doubt that the global economic and financial system has been radically transformed since the Bretton Woods Conference and the establishment of the World Bank and its sister institutions. Three developments are worth noting:

◆   Several developing countries have grown rapidly and have reached a stage of development not much below that of the industrialised world. If multilateral development banks played a role in the performance of these 'miracle economies' it was, at best, a marginal one.

◆   Trade has become a larger part of global product, with the developing world having secured important positions as suppliers of a number of important products. Resources generated in export markets have been much more important stimulants of economic growth in a number of successful countries than the capital flows provided by the multilateral development banks (MDBs).

◆   Development of global finance has brought a number of developing countries into the financial markets. They have begun to receive large amounts of capital flows without the need for intermediation by official development banks. Today, private capital flows are more than five times the flow of official development assistance, including lending by MDBs.

[1]The author is the Chief Executive Officer of EMP-Financial Advisors. Before he took up his present position in October 1999, he was at the World Bank. His last two positions at the World Bank were Vice President of Latin America and the Caribbean (January 1994–August 1999) and Director of the China and Mongolia Department (May 1987–January 1994).

Do these changes in the structure of world economy imply a radical re-definition of the role of multilateral development institutions? Do these developments mean that the MDBs, having lost their original *raison d'être*, have become largely redundant? These questions have been asked for many years – by the Brandt Commission in the early 1980s; by a group of non-governmental organisations in the mid-1990s; and, more recently, by the commission headed by Alan Meltzer. The Brandt Commission recommended refocusing development assistance on poverty alleviation. The NGOs, gathering under the umbrella of 'fifty years is enough', pro-posed the abolition of development banks and the IMF. The Meltzer Commission, convened by the US Congress, has suggested a significant change in the organisation and mandate of international financial insti-tutions, including the World Bank.

Since the Meltzer Commission is the most recent exercise, we will discuss its recommendations at some length. The Commission's suggestions draw upon a simple three-point logic that could be summed up as follows:

◆ Since many developing countries have reasonable access to inter-national financial markets, they do not need multinational develop-ment bank financing. They should not, therefore, receive any fund-ing from these institutions, at least not from the World Bank. If any MDB assistance is to flow to these creditworthy countries, it should come from regional banks such as the Inter-American Development Bank (IADB) and the Asian Development Bank (ADB).

◆ Since there are still a very large number of poor countries in the world with no immediate prospect of gaining access to world finan-cial markets, and since these countries have very little capacity to save, they need external capital flows. These flows, coming in as loans, create repayment problems and a very heavy burden of debt. Poor countries should, therefore, be provided with grants.

◆ To clear the decks for the poor countries, the debt they have accumulated from both multilateral and bilateral sources should be written off.

Following this logic, the Meltzer Commission proposed the following changes in the way the World Bank and two regional banks, the Inter-American Development Bank and the Asian Development Bank, con-duct their business:

◆ The Development Banks should be renamed Development Agencies;

◆ All resource transfers to countries with either an investment-grade bond rating or per capita income of $4000 should be phased out over a period of five years;

◆   In poor countries without capital market access (less than $4000 per capita income *and* a junk bond rating), MDB loans and guarantees for infrastructure and social services should be replaced by grants;

◆   The Development Agencies should be precluded from crisis lending, which should be made the sole responsibility of the IMF;

◆   All World Bank country and regional programmes in Latin America and Asia should be transferred to the IADB and ADB respectively, also within a period of five years;

◆   The World Bank should become the principal source of aid (*aid, not loans, investment or guarantees*) for Africa until the African Development Bank is ready to take full responsibility;

◆   The World Development Agency should concentrate on the provision of global and regional public goods (i.e. measures to help counter the effects of AIDS, protect the environment, promote best practices, build inter-country infrastructure, etc.);

◆   Some of the World Development Agency's callable capital should be reallocated to the regional development agencies and some should be reduced (presumably returned to shareholders);

◆   The Development Agencies should no longer provide investment, loans or guarantees to the private sector. The International Finance Corporation (IFC) should be merged into the World Development Agency and its capital base should be returned to shareholders. Likewise, the Inter-American Investment Corporation (IIC) should be merged with the IADB, and its capital base should be absorbed by the IADB. The Multilateral Investment Guarantee Agency (MIGA) should be eliminated;

◆   The World Bank and regional development banks should write off in their entirety their claims against all heavily indebted poor countries that implement an effective development strategy under the banks' combined supervision.

This paper argues that the Commission's logic does not necessarily lead to the structural changes proposed by it. To focus on the future evolution of the MDBs, we should first look at the way they have developed since their establishment. In terms of their structure and the areas they seek to reach, the MDBs are very different institutions today from those envisaged by their founding fathers at Bretton Woods. In arriving at their present situation they have passed several milestones. Of these the following eight are worth noting:

The switch from reconstruction to development. This occurred quickly as first Europe, and then Japan, quickly recovered from the ravages of World War II. The countries in Europe that had created large colonial empires with-drew from Asia and Africa, giving independence to scores of new nations. Some of these countries were seen as sufficiently creditworthy to borrow from multilateral development banks. Accordingly, the World Bank and two regional banks, the IADB and the ADB, developed large lending programmes in several newly independent countries.

Creation of the International Development Association (IDA), as a soft-lending arm of the World Bank. This resulted from the recognition that even the large countries of South Asia – India and Pakistan – were only marginally creditworthy to borrow large amounts of funds from multilateral institutions. They needed less burdensome sources of development finance. Initially, developing countries wished to create a soft-loan institution under the auspices of the UN. To be called SUNFED, this institution, with a one-country one-vote mode of governance, would have been more responsive to the developing world. Instead, the donor community agreed to establish the IDA as a World Bank associate. IDA's governance gave a greater voice to the donors, as compared to the borrowers.

Creation of the International Finance Corporation (IFC). The recognition that the private sector has an important developmental role dates back to the 1950s and led to the creation of the IFC as a World Bank affiliate. Unlike the parent World Bank, the IFC does not receive government guarantees for lending to the private sector.

The move from infrastructure to more broad-based development. Initial thinking on development was influenced by the success of the reconstruction efforts in Europe where investment in rebuilding physical infrastructure paid off handsomely. Accordingly, multilateral development banks initially focused their resources on large infrastructure projects. Roads, bridges, railways, ports and irrigation systems received large amounts of funding. However, as empirical evidence began to be gathered and analysed, it became clear that development needed a more broad-based approach. Industry and agriculture in particular needed funds and these were provided through development finance corporations (DFCs). The DFCs, working primarily as intermediaries, were supposed to replicate the work of the multilateral development banks. They received funds from the MDBs and provided these to the private sector in industry and agriculture.

The focus on poverty. Two decades of MDB involvement in development did not produce dramatic results in either accelerating growth or allevi-ating poverty. In the early 1970s, the development community began to focus attention on poverty alleviation. There was consensus that the trickle down approach had not worked – the poor had not benefited even in countries where growth had been rapid. Rather than wait for growth to have an impact on poverty and improve the welfare of the poor, attention was increasingly paid to direct intervention to alleviate poverty. The World Bank, in particular, began to focus its resources on the sectors on which the poor depended for their livelihood. Rural and urban development became the favoured approach towards improving the condition of the poor. Later, following the 'basic needs approach', the World Bank and other development agencies brought other sectors into their expanding portfolios. It was now understood that without improving the quality of human capital, the poor would not reap much benefit from the emphasis on rural and urban development.

The focus on macro-economic stability. While the direct focus on poverty was still being experimented with by the MDBs, the attention of the development community moved throughout the 1980s to the problem created by the debt crisis in Latin America. During this period, the development community arrived at a new agreement on the dynamics of development. Termed 'the Washington Consensus', since it represented the collective views of the Washington-based multilateral financial institutions and some think tanks, this approach emphasised economic openness and macro-economic stability (objectives that had previously been left to the IMF). In instituting this change in focus, the Bank developed new lending instruments – most notably, the Structural Adjustment Loan (SAL). Unlike traditional project loans, SALs produce not roads, clinics or power grids, but something intangible – the means to facilitate changes in policy. Consequently, it is more difficult to identify the net result of a SAL than that of a project loan. A number of structural adjustment programmes were devised and funded by the IFIs. In these programmes poverty alleviation and concerns about income distribution were put on the back-burner. The policies associated with the Washington Consensus had their most profound impact on the countries of Latin America. They brought about stability by eliminating hyper-inflation. Notwithstanding this success, this approach to development did not restore growth, reduce the incidence of poverty and improve income distribution.

New fiduciary responsibilities and safeguards. In the late 1980s and early 1990s the growing power of the civil society movement resulted in mounting pressure on the MDBs to introduce 'safeguard' policies aimed at preserving physical environment, protecting the livelihood of the people likely to be affected or displaced by development projects, and preserving native cultures. The MDBs used their considerable leverage to promote these safeguards in implementing their own programmes.

141

Expansion of the mandates (*corruption, governance, partnership, etc.*) *carried out with new instruments* (*Adaptable Program Loan* (*APL*), *Learning and Innovation Loan* (*LIL*), *Comprehensive Development Framework* (*CDF*), etc.). In the late 1990s, led by the World Bank's new management and prompted further by civil society, the multilateral banks began to take cognisance of the quality of governance among their clients. Corruption, rampant in several areas of the world, received special attention and, as was the case with the safeguards associated with environment, resettlement and native cultures, the MDBs put their clients on notice that good governance was expected of them.

Given the way the MDBs have evolved over time, are they relevant in today's world or do they need to be changed in many significant ways? This question is at the heart of the current debate on the role and relevance of these institutions. The Meltzer Commission reached two important conclusions. The first was that given the dramatic change in the global economic and financial system, the World Bank had largely lost its relevance. The second was that even if the Bank's mission, as recently reinterpreted, is accepted as a reason for its continued survival in its present form, it is not a good enough reason for not introducing significant changes. Alan Meltzer, the chairman of the commission that is referred to by his name, is not impressed with the MDBs' performance in the area of poverty. As he has pointed out: 'the percentage living in poverty is approximately the same as 40 years ago; the absolute number has doubled'.

In disagreeing with both conclusions, this paper takes an entirely different view. It argues that the MDBs have as important a role to play in today's world as they did when the World Bank – the most senior of the MDBs – was originally conceived. As demonstrated above, the MDBs have shown the capacity to change with the times; they should be able to do so again as the process of globalisation transforms the global financial and economic system in a very profound way.

There are three additional questions that need to be asked in order to determine whether the MDBs still have a role to play. Firstly, what are the changes that have occurred as a result of globalisation that need to be looked at in determining the future direction of the MDBs? Secondly, in a world dominated by the private sector, is there a role for publicly owned institutions such as the World Bank and the regional development banks? Thirdly, given the growing diversity of the developing world, can the role of a development bank be performed by a multilateral system dominated by one large institution such as the World Bank? Let us take up each of these questions in turn.

Globalisation: Globalisation is a complex process with many facets. The one that most impresses those who see multilateral development banks as increasingly irrelevant – or, if not irrelevant, at least marginal – is the enormous increase in private capital flows to the developing world. These flows now dwarf the money lent by MDBs. The fact that these flows are concentrated in a few countries does not deter the detractors of MDBs. They maintain that if a dozen or so countries account for approximately 80 per cent of private capital flows, then it should be recognised that the population of developing countries is similarly concentrated in a few large countries. In fact, as the Meltzer report emphasises, development bank lending is similarly concentrated in these same countries – a fact that unnerves the authors of that report. The Meltzer Commission recommends that the MDBs withdraw from lending to these emerging markets, and instead concentrate solely on the poorest countries that lack access to private capital and, because of their small size, are home to a relatively small proportion of the world's poor. Furthermore, it proposes that MDB involvement in the poorest countries should be constrained to grant-giving; multilateral lending would be abandoned. There are a number of flaws in this approach. Some of them (though certainly not all) are addressed below, first in the context of emerging markets, and then in the context of the poorer developing countries (defined as those with sub-investment-grade bond ratings and per capita income of below $2500).

Three points are relevant with respect to the emerging markets. Firstly, MDB lending to these countries is counter-cyclical, whereas private capital flows are strongly pro-cyclical and disappear when they are most needed. The argument that MDB financing to these sectors/regions simply replaces government spending does not hold at a time when most fiscal and other constraints severely curtail the spending capacity of governments. Secondly, MDB lending reaches sectors and regions within these nations that private capital does not. Socioeconomic and financial returns to capital often differ sharply, but private capital is not the least bit interested in socioeconomic returns. Thirdly, MDB loans, insurance and guarantees catalyse private capital that would not, in the absence of MDB resources, reach these countries due to imperfections in the private financial markets. Despite the impressive growth in resources controlled by the private capital markets, these markets are far from perfectly efficient. The volume of capital flows alone tells us nothing about the efficiency of the markets. Investors continue to move in herds and there are certain risks that the private sector is still unwilling to accept.

With respect to the developing countries, there are also three points which should be stressed. Firstly, despite the assertions of the Meltzer Commission, the switch to grant giving would jeopardise and politicise – and thus, compromise – the allocation of overseas development aid, as the development banks would be entirely dependent on increasingly budget-conscious donor governments. Secondly, the switch would compromise efforts to build a 'credit culture' in these countries. Thirdly, the Meltzer Commission strongly discourages the allocation of MDB resources to countries with poor governance. But poor countries, almost by definition, lack good governance.[1] The withdrawal of MDB resources would not, in all likelihood, improve governance in countries where political and economic power is highly concentrated. Instead, the poor in these countries would be further marginalised.

Privatisation of capital flows: It is suggested that international financial markets' willingness to invest large amounts of capital in many parts of the developing world has reduced the original role of MDBs as financial intermediaries. The proponents of this view emphasise that capital markets have shown that they can operate in developing countries without the need for intermediation. There are a number of flaws in this line of thinking. The most obvious is that it treats private and public flows as substitutable, assuming that if there is a great deal of the latter then there is not much need for the former. It has been shown in the past that in many countries MDBs' close involvement with the process and direction of development created the environment in which the private sector could operate with profit. The following counter-factual could be suggested: if the MDBs had not acted as they did, private capital flows would not have reached the same level.

The second flaw in this line of thinking is that whereas private flows can be – and in fact in many situations have been – volatile, the services provided by the MDBs have come in a relatively stable stream. At times, the MDBs have acted in a counter-cyclical way, dampening the volatility caused by the sudden arrival and/or departure of private money.

The World Bank's dominance in the structure of multilateral development finance: It is arguable that the present MDB structure, with the World Bank having a global mandate, the regional development banks serving specific regional priorities and sub-regional banks dealing with the development problems of specific geographical regions, does not need to be changed dramatically. The system has evolved over a period of more than five decades in response to the challenges it has faced from time to time. With some adjustment, the system could deal with the opportunities created by globalisation, while helping the developing world to cope with the volatility associated with the increasing globalisation of financial markets.

---

[1] Forty of 41 low-income countries studied in the World Bank's 1998 *Annual Review of Development Effectiveness* are characterised by inadequate governance.

What additional changes could be made in the way the World Bank currently operates? This paper puts forward four suggestions:

◆ The Bank should concentrate on project lending, but should undertake projects within the framework of country and/or sectoral programmes. The justification for financing projects should not simply be on the basis of acceptable rates of economic and financial returns.

◆ The Bank should concentrate its resources in areas in which borrowers can benefit from its global experience, leaving other projects to be financed by the regional banks.

◆ In the sectors in which private capital is available, the Bank should work closely with institutions such as private equity funds. Clearly, synergies could arise from greater collaboration between private equity funds and the MDBs, as both are important suppliers of finance to the developing world. World Bank country, regional and sectoral expertise could assist these funds in their work. This relationship should be sustained over the long run.

◆ The Bank should leave structural adjustment lending to the IMF.

In conclusion, this paper emphasises the following point. There has been a dramatic change in the structure of the global economy; this change should be factored into the way multilateral development institutions such as the World Bank operate. However, the World Bank has shown an impressive capacity to change and further evolution in its structure and operational policies would enable it to retain its relevance. The Bank and the regional institutions created in its image still have a significant role to play.

Systemic Reform at a Standstill: A Flock of 'G's in Search of Global Financial Stability

Roy Culpeper[1]

Introduction

The subject of 'global governance' became topical in the 1990s with a rash of financial crises, the most far-reaching and dramatic one having started in East Asia in mid-1997 and spread around the world before subsiding during the course of 1999. It is worth recalling, however, that global governance has been a hardy perennial since the breakdown of the original Bretton Woods system a quarter of a century ago. Its antecedents include the debate on the New International Economic Order in the 1970s; the North-South Summits of the early 1980s; the UNCED negotiations in Rio de Janeiro in 1992; and the chain of ensuing UN conferences throughout the decade – the Vienna conference on human rights, the social summit at Copenhagen, the Beijing conference on gender and development, and the Cairo conference on population and development. While these discussions have produced a few tangible results, their impact on global governance has been minimal. Although it may sound unpleasant to believers in the rationality of a more equitable world order, perhaps a large reason for the failure of these many attempts to reform the global order is that they have been dominated by the poor and the powerless, while the rich and powerful have not been persuaded of the need for significant changes to the status quo.

Yet, there are signs that the acquiescence in the global status quo of the world's rich and powerful countries may be changing. The financial crises of the 1990s demonstrated that the emerging global capital market, due to various imperfections, is critically vulnerable to systemic failure. Financial crises in Mexico, in East Asia, and in Brazil, Russia and many other parts of the world during 1994–99 accompanied unprecedented volatility in international capital flows, gyrations in exchange rates and accompanying turmoil in financial markets (Fischer, 1999a: F557–F561). Accordingly, in the depths of the last crisis (around September 1998), there were calls by the leaders of the Group of Seven (G-7) industrial

---

[1]The author is grateful to his colleague John Serieux for comments on an earlier draft of this paper.

powers to 'reform the global financial architecture'. Given that, this time, it is the world's most powerful countries, rather than coalitions of developing countries, seeking to reform global governance is there greater likelihood than in the past that meaningful change will occur?

Systemic failure warrants systemic reform. Yet the character of the reforms initiated since 1998 may be considered, at best, as shoring up the defences of countries entering the global financial markets, in order to reduce their vulnerabilities to systemic failure. A preliminary assessment leads to the conclusion that the reforms to date comprise small, perhaps tiny, steps in the right direction. As Stanley Fischer, First Deputy Managing Director of the IMF, put it recently, the changes contemplated would 'reform but not revolutionise the global financial system' (Fischer, 1999a). To use an architectural metaphor, the scope of reforms currently being undertaken amounts to repairs (albeit important ones) rather than extensive rebuilding, let alone the construction of new edifices. The plumbers and roofers, so to speak, have taken over. The problem is that such modest repairs are not likely to be enough to prepare the world for the systemic financial crises that may be yet to come. Moreover, the reforms being undertaken are asymmetric: they are heavily weighted towards policy changes required of borrowers and debtors, while much less onus is put on lenders and creditors. Accordingly, future crises are increasingly likely to be generated by policy imbalances in or among the world's richest countries rather than in the 'emerging markets'.

This paper critically surveys what has been achieved to date under the leadership of the world's great economic powers. It is organised as follows. The next section briefly sets the context by examining current prospects for the global economy in the wake of the most recent round of financial crises. It then considers the accomplishments and shortcomings of the 'flock of Gs' – the various groups formed by the leading industrial countries since 1960 to oversee international monetary co-operation and reform. These evolved with the changing conditions and challenges posed by a steadily integrating global economy. As a result of the recent Asian financial crisis, two key new institutions were created to spearhead the latest round of reforms, the Financial Stability Forum (FSF) and the Group of 20 (G-20). The subsequent section makes a critical examination of the scope of the reforms being considered by the FSF and G-20. The final section reflects on key systemic challenges that are not being addressed, as well as the possibility of strengthening regional approaches to reform of the global financial architecture.

The focus of the paper is on the issue of how to achieve or restore financial stability in a globalising and increasingly sophisticated capital market.

While the paper dwells principally on the more advanced developing countries and 'emerging markets', it does not delve into issues related to the needs of the poorest countries and people in the emerging global system. Such issues, while at least as crucial as those examined here, raise somewhat different sorts of questions and answers, cogently addressed in a recent Overseas Development Council report (2000) on the IMF and by Griffith-Jones, Ocampo and Cailloux (1999). The author has attempted to address these issues elsewhere in a paper on the implications of financial instability for long-term development financing (Culpeper, 1999).

The Context: Life after the 'Asian Crisis'

According to estimates made during the first quarter of 2000, recovery from the global economic downturn precipitated by the Asian crisis in 1997–98 has been more robust than expected. Global growth in 1999 was 3.3 per cent, some 50 per cent higher than the growth rate projected at the end of 1998 (IMF, 2000a:1). Growth forecasts for the developing countries have also been revised upwards in the years 2000 (by 0.4 per cent to 4.6 per cent) and 2001–2 (by 0.1 per cent to 4.8 per cent) (World Bank, 2000: 2).

Recovery in the crisis-afflicted countries has been spurred by trade and foreign direct investment, fuelled by buoyant growth in the industrial countries, particularly North America. Whether the unpredicted vigour of the 'V-shaped recovery' is due to the IMF-led adjustment and stabilisation efforts adopted by the emerging market countries, as claimed by the IMF (IMF, 2000a:4), or to other underlying factors, should be the subject of debate for some time to come.

Despite the strong economic recovery in 1999, both globally and in the emerging markets, private flows from capital markets to developing countries continued their retreat, to levels last seen in the early 1990s. The conspicuous exception was foreign direct investment, which remained resilient through the crisis years, to become the single largest source of long-term finance at a record $192 billion, compared to $35 billion in 1991 and $131 billion in 1996 (World Bank, 2000:3).

Notwithstanding the pleasantly surprising recovery, there is reason to express concern about the outlook for the next decade. First and foremost, speedy recovery from crisis is the handmaiden of complacency. Lessons learned will soon be forgotten as the severity of the crisis is attenuated in the minds of those who should know better, and incentives to seek long-term solutions are dulled. But, particularly if the global recovery continues for a few years at its current vigorous pace, a repetition of the volatile capital flows and boom-bust cycle experienced by some parts of the world is altogether likely. Presumably, if the reform initiatives launched in 1999–2000 are widely implemented in the emerging market countries, these countries might be better able to prevent financial crises or become less likely to be affected by contagion from other countries. The question, however, is whether such measures will be enough, and whether remedies for larger systemic crises will be in place.

In this context, the area of greatest concern is perhaps the outlook for the world's major economies. In particular, the US current account deficit is at record levels, alongside persistently large surpluses in Japan. The US current account deficit, which ran at an annualised rate of $400 billion in the last quarter of 1999, now exceeds the previous record of 3.4 per cent of GDP reached in 1985–86 (a time of currency disequilibrium and uncertainty, resolved for a time by the Plaza and Louvre Accords). Current forecasts indicate a further rise in the US current deficit over the next two years to unprecedented levels.[1] The mirror image of the growing current account deficit is the continuing growth of US private debt and borrowing, also at record levels; private net saving became negative in 1996 and now stands below −5 per cent of GDP (IMF, 2000:9, fig.1.2).

This lopsided pattern in the world's principal currency areas is unlikely to be sustainable, judging from recent and past experience. Two related factors are the persistent overvaluation of the US dollar relative to the euro, and the unprecedentedly high stock market valuations in the USA and elsewhere. A significant risk exists of sudden changes in market sentiment toward the US dollar and stock prices, with the possibility of very disruptive realignments and corrections, which could well spill over into a major recession in the industrial countries and around the world (IMF, 2000a:4). Ironically, the USA may be subject to the same sequence of events besetting Asia in 1997–98: a sudden reversal of the inflow with massive capital flight, along with rapid currency depreciation and asset deflation, including a stock market 'meltdown'. This time, however, world recovery may not be around the corner, as the scope for offsetting policy initiatives by other countries is far more limited than in 1998 or in 1985, when the world's major currencies were last egregiously misaligned (Krugman, 1999a).

These particular threats to global economic stability are mentioned here because they now present the major challenges to the world's financial

---

[1] According to the IMF, the US current account *deficit*, at 2.5 per cent of GDP in 1998 and 3.7 per cent in 1999, is forecast to rise to 4.3 per cent in 2000 and 4.4 per cent in 2001. The corresponding data for Japan are a *surplus* of 3.2 per cent (1998), 2.5 per cent (1999), 2.2 per cent (2000) and 2.3 per cent (2001) (IMF, 2000a:5, Table 1.2).

architecture – challenges that are as yet barely on the reform agenda and thus represent its greatest shortcoming.

The Evolution of Global Financial Governance

The post-war era has given birth to a host of deliberative fora within which international monetary and economic co-operation have been discussed – the G-10, the G-7/G-8, the G-24, the G-22 and, most recently, the G-20. To this 'gaggle of Gs' can be added the recently-created Financial Stability Forum. While none of these groupings has any operational or implementation capability, what they all have in common (with the notable exception of the G-24) is membership of the world's most economically powerful countries or, in the more euphemistic jargon of today, the most 'systemically significant' nation-states.

Therein lies their importance. A review of the past indicates that nothing consequential happens in the formally constituted international organisations that do have operational capabilities – the IMF, the World Bank, the Bank for International Settlements (BIS) – without the prior consent, and usually the active endorsement, of the 'Gs' (here used as a short form for all the deliberative groups and committees dominated by the major industrial countries). Therefore, the overall policy direction chosen by the flock of Gs has a major impact on the formal institutional infrastructure – both as to its scope and its detailed activities. Couched in terms of the debate over the last two years on the 'global financial architecture', the reform of the international financial system has essentially been determined by these deliberative bodies.

A brief history

The Bretton Woods Institutions (BWIs) – the International Monetary Fund and the World Bank – were created at the end of World War II to provide a framework of institutional co-operation that would promote relatively stable exchange rates, growth in trade and commerce, and development of the world's poorest countries. The BWIs were deliberately designed in such a way that the economically more powerful members had a greater voice and vote within them. But the influence of the economically powerful countries, from very early on in the post-war period, was by no means restricted to the BWIs. A series of fora was established outside the BWIs in which the world's leading industrial powers were the exclusive members.

The first such forum was the Group of 10 (G-10), formed in 1961 to supplement the resources of the IMF through the General Arrangements to

Borrow (GAB). The G-10 evolved from Working Party 3 of the OECD, consisting of finance ministry and central bank officials from the ten largest OECD member countries[1] plus Switzerland.

The crucial significance of the establishment in the 1960s of the G-10 for the subsequent evolution of global financial governance cannot be under-estimated. The GAB was explicitly designed by the G-10 to circumvent the need of the richest industrial countries to seek balance of payments financing exclusively from the IMF. As historian Harold James put it, the main attraction of the GAB for the USA and UK was that 'it would be speedy and non-interventionist. It would bring money quickly without "advice" or control from multilateral agencies.' In other words, the GAB provided the G-10 countries with an escape hatch from the IMF.

Agreement was reached among the ten to provide up to $6 billion to members of the group to forestall or cope with an impairment of the inter-national monetary system. Soon, however, the GAB aroused the sus-picion that a new ideology of co-operation between industrial countries had replaced the universalist aspirations of Bretton Woods. The G-10 seemed a very exclusive club, dividing the world into haves and have-nots; conspicuously absent were representatives of the developing coun-tries, many of which were just emerging from colonialism. Indeed, serious discussion about how to manage the international monetary system shifted during the 1960s to this new forum, with the developing dollar glut and gold shortage, and the rise of the Euromarkets, much to the chagrin of the IMF, whose Managing Director believed it should host and oversee this debate (James, 1996:161–5).

During the 1960s discussions among G-10 Finance Ministers, and the work undertaken by the G-10 deputies (senior officials of central banks and finance ministries), eerily anticipated similar preoccupations in the 1990s. There were talks about how to generate liquidity for use in emer-gency situations (resulting in the creation of Special Drawing Rights in 1968), and recommendations about the need for an 'early warning system' to head off serious currency crises (turmoil in the 1990s resulted in the creation of the IMF's Special Data Dissemination Standard for this very purpose).

Notwithstanding the similarity of members of the G-10 – they were all advanced industrialised countries – there were also important schisms in this group almost from the beginning. In particular, the USA balked at the heavy representation of Europeans in the group (comprising seven of the

---

[1]The G-10 comprised the G-7 (USA, Japan, Germany, France, Italy, UK and Canada) plus the Netherlands, Belgium and Sweden. Switzerland later joined the G-10.

ten). Accordingly, in its discussions the G-10 only went so far: it was blocked by the Americans from exercising any surveillance over the policies of its members and the discussion of the dollar was off-limits (James, 1996:183).

The dollar crisis of 1971, again reminiscent of problems in the mid-1980s and late 1990s, was preceded by growing current account deficits in the USA. With the suspension of the dollar's convertibility into gold in August, the Bretton Woods fixed exchange-rate system came to an end. There ensued a series of failed discussions aimed at reforming the international monetary system, principally by trying to restore the fixed parities at new equilibrium rates. In the increasingly chaotic setting of the 1970s, the G-10 was convened many times, but was unable to function as a deliberative forum to reach viable agreement[1] on a new system. The Americans increasingly found the G-10 to be an unsuitable forum to discuss systemic reform, and in securing outcomes sought by the USA.

Meanwhile, between September 1972 and June 1974, a 'Committee of 20' (C-20), based on the membership of the IMF Executive Board (with representation at ministerial level rather than by officials as on the Board), took up the challenge of reform. Unlike the G-10, the C-20 was more universal, and significantly included representation of the developing countries. But its deliberations were encumbered by the large number of participants (three from each country plus advisers) and feeble secretariat support. Moreover, discussions on whether and how to reform the system, including the objective of a return to fixed exchange-rate parities, were difficult and hamstrung by continuing differences between the current account deficit-ridden USA, on the one hand, and Japan and Germany (both in current account surplus), on the other. The oil price crisis of 1973 further complicated matters by sparking a world-wide cycle of inflation that was not extinguished for over a decade.

Regrettably for those to whom the C-20 seemed a more inclusive and universal body (than, say, the G-10) in which to deliberate on global monetary reform, the experiment ended in failure, or at any rate without resolving the long-term problems that had led to the demise of the post-war exchange-rate system (Williamson, 1977; Mohammed, 1996). After its last meeting in June 1974 the C-20 had to acknowledge its inability to return the world to a stable and fixed (but adjustable) exchange parity system (James, 1996:256). The lasting impact of the C-20 was to transform itself into the policy-deliberating Interim Committee, and eventually, in 1999, into the International Monetary and Financial Committee, a

---

[1]With the possible exception of the Smithsonian Agreement of December 1971, which broke down over the next year.

more inclusive ministerial body than the G-10 before it or the G-7 after it. Soon after the creation of the Interim Committee, a parallel 'Development Committee' was set up, comprising mostly the same members, but focused on long-term resource flows to developing countries. In contrast, the Interim Committee deliberated on issues concerning short-term balance of payments financing and adjustment policy for borrowers requiring access to such short-term financing.

The American aversion towards the G-10 had in the meantime led increasingly to bilateral discussions on international financial issues with France, Japan and Germany. Eventually, a more informal group, the G-5 (comprising Finance Ministers and Central Bank Governors from the USA, Japan, Germany, France and the UK), began to meet as the 'Library Group' from March 1973 and continued to meet until 1986, when it was superseded by the G-7 (with the addition of Italy and Canada). And at Rambouillet, France in November 1975, the first Economic Summit was convened for heads of government of the G-6 (the G-5 plus Italy). The second such summit was hosted in Puerto Rico by the USA and, at the Americans' insistence, Canada was invited to join. In the new group, European countries comprised four out of the seven, rather than eight out of the eleven in the G-10 (including Switzerland). In this new setting, the Americans had fewer problems dealing with a united European front, and the group's *modus operandi* was also far less formal. The G-7 was born.

The G-10 was superseded by the G-7 as the pre-eminent forum for the largest industrial countries. However, instead of disappearing, the G-10 began to play a different role, one focused more on relationships built around the BIS in Basle (the original venue where the GAB was actually negotiated) (Griffith-Jones and Kimmis, 1999:29–30). Now primarily a forum for Central Bank Governors, the G-10 has recently been pivotal to discussions on financial stability and regulation, which emerged dramatically during the Asian financial crisis (see below).

Although the key participants in the G-7 summits were government leaders, and their agenda was eventually caught up with political issues, the original intention was to deliberate on key economic issues. Hence, the Finance Ministers (and Central Bank Governors) have always been key players in the G-7. The centrality of Finance Ministers to the G-7 process has been evident since the 1986 Tokyo Summit. Since that time, the G-7 Finance Deputies have developed their own rhythm of consultation throughout the year (Bayne and Putnam, 1995).

The power of the G-7 to shape the international rules of the game soon became apparent. The Rambouillet Summit endorsed floating exchange rates that had become the *de facto* system since the breakdown of the short-lived Smithsonian agreement. Soon after, in January 1976, the G-7's proposals were accepted by the new Interim Committee and led subsequently to the Second Amendment of the IMF's Articles of Agreement. The latter sought to promote a 'stable system of exchange rates' (that is, floating rates responsibly managed) rather than a 'system of stable exchange rates' (as under the moribund Bretton Woods system).

For the next quarter of a century, the G-7 dominated global financial governance, as it continues to do today. However, it is quite evident that during its first decade, the G-7 members were mostly preoccupied by frictions among themselves, particularly regarding exchange-rate relationships and balance of payments financing. In the late 1970s attention was focused on financing the current account deficits of the UK and Italy, via both the soft-conditionality GAB and hard-conditionality IMF (these turned out to be the last major IMF programmes among the developed countries). Then, in the 1980s, with the US dollar trading at unsustainably high levels against the yen and D-mark, much of the energy of the G-7 was consumed in discussions leading to the Plaza Accord (1985) and the Louvre Accord (1987) on currency co-ordination.

In contrast with its preoccupation over exchange rates, the onset of the developing country debt crisis in 1982 did not trigger intervention by the G-7 until the Baker Plan in 1985. That flawed initiative maintained that 100 per cent of the debt would be repaid. Emanating from US Treasury Secretary James Baker, it was an American scheme formulated in Washington and conveyed to G-7 partners, involving little prior collaborative discussion. The issue of third world debt was thereafter explicitly put on the G-7 summit agenda for the first time in 1986, although it had been secretly discussed at Williamsburg in 1983 (James, 1996: 390). The failed Baker Plan was followed in 1989 by the Brady Plan (Nicholas Brady was Baker's successor at the US Treasury), a far more successful initiative than its predecessor since it encouraged voluntary debt reduction. However, like the Baker Plan, it also seemed to involve little prior consultation with the G-7; rather it developed out of pilot projects with Wall Street firms (such as Morgan Guaranty Trust) involving discounted debt swaps with Mexico.

On the surface, throughout the 1980s, when it came to exercising global financial governance to deal with major issues such as the debt crisis, policy direction seemed to have reverted to the Bretton Woods Institutions, particularly the IMF and the two new ministerial-level committees that emerged from the C-20 discussions, the Interim and Development Committees. But in fact, during the Reagan and Bush administrations, the USA had a determining influence on decisions taken either through the ministerial committees or the Executive Boards. However, even though it is the largest shareholder, it would be impossible for the USA unilaterally to impose its will on the entire membership of the IMF or World Bank. But with the support of the G-7, it commands close to one-half of the total voting power. The G-7 thus provided a 'rubber stamp' for decisions already taken by the USA and, in turn, the Bretton Woods organisations rubber-stamped declarations of the G-7 (Kafka, 1994:215).

The only counterweight to the G-7 was the G-24, a committee of developing country finance ministers established in November 1971 when international monetary reform first moved to the forefront. The G-24 meets regularly before the scheduled meetings of the Interim and Development Committees and issues a communiqué in which the views of developing countries are put forward. However, while the G-24 has gradually developed a capacity to critique current policies and articulate cogent policy alternatives[1] to those being adopted under the aegis of the G-7, its influence on actual policy cannot be described as more than marginal.

The *modus operandi* of the G-7 established during the 1980s, in which the USA acted as the undisputed first among equals (a status reinforced by the demise of the Soviet Union), persisted well into the 1990s. The Mexican peso crisis of 1994–95 perhaps represented the last expression of US hegemonic initiative in this form. Involving a rapidly-assembled $50 billion bail-out package (of which $20 billion came from the USA and $17.7 billion from the IMF), the locus of the crisis clearly prompted the USA to act quickly and not get bogged down in consultations with G-7 partners, much to the irritation of the Europeans.

Although side discussions between the G-7 leaders and the Russian President began in 1991, it was not until the Naples Summit of 1994 that Russia was admitted as an equal partner, but only in the political discussions, which by then occupied half of the agenda of the heads of government. However, Russia was not admitted as an equal partner with the G-7 Finance Ministers; hence the schizophrenic summit designation since Naples of 'G7/G8'.

Recent developments

Even though the 1994–95 currency crisis was handled in ways reminiscent of the debt crisis of the preceding decade (with the USA taking the

---

[1]Particularly noteworthy is the research under the direction of Sidney Dell, Gerry Helleiner and (currently) Dani Rodrik, resulting *inter alia* in the multi-volume series *International Monetary and Financial Issues for the 1990s*, cited extensively in this paper.

initiative and the G-7, along with the international financial institutions, following suit) important signs emerged that the USA and the G-7 now recognised the need to involve other 'systemically significant' countries in the governance of the international financial system. This transpired for several reasons. The scale of the intervention in Mexico was histori-cally unprecedented. The capacity of the IMF, even with an increase in resources anticipated from the Eleventh Quota Review, would have been severely stretched to meet other such exigencies. Global financial market integration was proceeding at an accelerating pace. With the rapid growth of cross-border portfolio equity and derivatives markets, as well as short-term bank lending, greater uncertainty and unpredictability than ever was attached to surges in international capital flows. Perhaps not the least significant factor was that the US dollar was itself caught up in the currency turmoil of 1995.

Accordingly, at the 1995 Halifax Summit, the G-7 countries resolved to mobilise additional emergency funding, on the model of the General Arrangements to Borrow which had been in existence for 33 years. Financing available under the GAB, which had been renewed every four or five years and utilised on ten occasions (including for the UK and Italy in the late 1970s), was augmented to SDR17 billion (about US$23 billion) in 1982. At Halifax, the G-7 sought to supplement funding through the GAB, but from a larger body of creditors, including the 'emerging market' countries. Including the 12 original G-10 members involved in the GAB, the New Arrangements to Borrow (NAB) now comprised 25 participants and added a further SDR17 billion to the resources available under the GAB, to make a total of SDR34 billion (about $46 billion).[1]

As with the GAB, the NAB was formally established through a decision of the IMF Executive Board, in January 1997, and it became effective in November 1998. Also consistent with the policy endorsed for the GAB, a proposal for calls on the NAB by the IMF's Managing Director can become effective only if it is accepted by the NAB participants, and the proposal is then approved by the Executive Board.[2]

The NAB, which emerged from the Mexican peso crisis, was the precursor of the G-7 initiatives launched in the wake of the ensuing Asian

---

[1] The members of the NAB included the G-10 plus Australia, Austria, Denmark, Finland, Hong Kong Monetary Authority, Korea, Kuwait, Luxembourg, Malaysia, Norway, Singapore, Spain and Thailand. Saudi Arabia, which had previously been an associate member of the GAB, was also a member of the NAB.

[2] When this paper was written, the NAB had been called upon once, to finance an IMF programme for Brazil in December 1998.

financial crisis which erupted in Thailand in July 1997. These initiatives have further widened the scope of discourse on global financial governance. The first step was taken by the USA at a summit meeting of APEC leaders in Vancouver in November 1997. That meeting generated an invitation by US President Bill Clinton to Finance Ministers from a group of 'systemically significant' economies. The 'Group of 22' met in Washington in February (at the Willard Hotel, thus the nickname 'Willard Group') and again in April 1998 as the crisis continued to deepen in Asia and spread to other parts of the world. Its purpose, according to US Treasury Secretary Robert Rubin, was to examine issues related to the stability of the international financial system and the effective functioning of global capital markets.

The membership of the G-22 was never quite settled and remained somewhat fluid for the duration of its work. But significantly, in addition to the G-7, it included members of the industrial, transition and developing countries, reminiscent of the C-20 in the early 1970s. There, however, the resemblance stopped. The agenda of the G-22 was far more focused on the minutiae of financial instability rather than on reforming the 'architecture' of the global financial system. To wit, its efforts were organised under three working groups – the first on enhancing transparency and accountability; the second on strengthening financial systems; and the third on managing financial crises.

Nonetheless, the G-22 has had a significant impact on shaping – perhaps limiting is a more accurate description – the reform efforts that followed. In October 1998 the three working groups submitted their reports. The report on enhancing transparency and accountability recommended that the IMF prepare a Transparency Report summarising the extent to which an economy meets internationally recognised disclosure standards, presaging the Reports on Observance of Standards and Codes (ROSCs) launched by the IMF early in 1999. The report on strengthening financial systems recommended, among other things, the establishment of a Financial Sector Policy Forum to discuss sector issues, foreshadowing the Financial Stability Forum which first met in April 1999. The group on managing financial crises perhaps had the most formidable task, but contented itself with setting out principles and features of regimes facilitating rapid and orderly work-outs from excessive indebtedness, and exhorted countries to 'make the strongest possible efforts to meet the terms and conditions of all debt contracts in full and on time' (US Department of the Treasury, 1998; IMF, 2000b).

By the time the G-22 reports were tabled at the IMF/World Bank Annual Meetings in October 1998, the G-7 was meeting to consider how to reform the international financial architecture in light of the discussion at the Birmingham Summit during the summer and statements made by UK Prime Minister Tony Blair and President Bill Clinton on the need for a 'new Bretton Woods'. To this end, G-7 Ministers and Central Bank Governors met in mid-September and twice in October. Hans Tietmeyer, the retiring Governor of the German Bundesbank (shortly to be superseded by the new European Central Bank), was commissioned to report on international co-operation and co-ordination in the area of financial market supervision and surveillance.

This flurry of activity resulted in Tietmeyer's report, which recommended establishing the Financial Stability Forum (see below).[1] The G-7 Ministers and Central Bank Governors also spelled out a 36-point 'Plan for Implementation' for the Global Financial Architecture, which was submitted to the G-7 Heads of Government in December 1998 (Group of Seven, 1999a). At the ensuing 1999 G-7 Köln Summit, there were calls for the establishment of an informal mechanism for discussions among a broad group of countries on the international financial system. When G-7 Finance Ministers and Central Bank Governors met in September 1999, the Group of 20 (G-20) was proposed as a new international forum consisting of Finance Ministers and Central Bank Governors representing 19 countries, as well as representatives of the European Union and the BWIs.[2] Its purpose was 'to ensure broader participation in discussions on international financial affairs among countries whose size or strategic importance gives them a particularly crucial role in the global economy'. Canada's Finance Minister, Paul Martin, was nominated as the G-20's first Chair. The first meeting of the G-20 was held in Berlin in December 1999.

The two vehicles crafted by the G-7 in 1999 – the FSF and the G-20 – are now the principal vehicles of international financial reform. For different reasons, explored in greater depth below, these two institutions have broken new ground with regard to the scope of participation. While it is important to acknowledge the advance they represent over the G-7, with respect to their inclusiveness and their legitimacy, it is also evident that they are still heavily dominated by the G-7. Moreover, the agendas they have embarked upon have all the hallmarks of previous reform

---

[1] The title of Tietmeyer's report, 'International co-operation and co-ordination in the area of financial market supervision and surveillance', is indicative of the narrow scope of his enquiry.

[2] In addition to the G-7, the following are represented on the G-20: Argentina, Australia, Brazil, China, India, Indonesia, Korea, Mexico, Russia, Saudi Arabia, South Africa, Turkey and the EU. The Bretton Woods Institutions are also represented by the IMF Managing Director, the World Bank President and the Chairman of the Development Committee.

attempts through the G-22, the G-7 and G-10 – attempts that have concentrated more on fine-tuning the details of the current global financial system rather than on addressing the most fundamental challenges posed by it.

Systemic Reform: Architects v. Plumbers

The financial crises of the 1990s have been the subject of considerable debate and analysis. A considerable degree of consensus has emerged as to the systemic nature of the problems (Mishkin, 1999; Krugman, 1999), if not the solutions.[1] However, it is possible, even at this point, to examine the kinds of solutions being contemplated by the FSF and the G-20, in order to determine whether they are likely to be *sufficient* to resolve the systemic problems.

What is to be reformed?

First, a short digression into the causes of emerging-market crises is necessary in order to distinguish the different kinds of solutions being proposed under the rubric of 'architectural reform'. Much of the analysis in the literature has dwelt on financial market imperfections. For example, problems of asymmetric information between borrowers and lenders leading to adverse selection (i.e. lending to the riskiest borrowers) and herding (bandwagon effects in which lenders follow the lead of others with little due diligence); self-fulfilling panics (herding in the opposite direction making a bad situation much worse); the possibility of multiple equilibria; and the lack of adequate bankruptcy mechanisms are all cited as causal factors underlying the crises (Rogoff, 1999). The fact of the matter is that these phenomena have been known for some time – much of the work of Hyman Minsky, for example, focused on the dynamics of financial instability (and the spillover of such instability into the real economy) arising from the fact that financial markets are *not* efficient (Kindleberger, 1996: 11).

The point, however, is that these phenomena pertain to *all* financial markets, and most financial markets are essentially *domestic*. Accordingly, the solutions, although not fail-safe, are largely domestic as well. They include greater transparency and disclosure by borrowers, supervision and regulation of the banking sector, bankruptcy mechanisms to settle creditors' claims when borrowers are illiquid or insolvent and a lender of last resort (usually the central bank). The world's most sophisticated financial

---

[1] See the numerous dissenting statements in the Goldstein and Meltzer Reports. Council on Foreign Relations, 1999; International Financial Institutions Commission, 2000.

markets, in the industrial countries, took many decades to develop the necessary institutions and infrastructure, and still experience widespread financial turmoil, for example the US savings and loan meltdown in the 1980s and widespread bank failure in Japan in the 1990s.

In other words, much of the 'architecture' necessary to contain potential financial turmoil is also essentially domestic. To the extent that financial markets become international, as they have over the past several decades, with lenders and borrowers situated in different countries, the possibility arises of devising international variants of these domestic solutions. Indeed, many analysts have proposed creating a new international lender of last resort, an international bankruptcy court, a world financial authority, an international deposit insurance corporation and so on (see Rogoff, 1999 for a quick summary).

But, with the possible exception of transforming the IMF from its current status as a revolving fund into a true international lender of last resort (Mohammed, 1999; Fischer, 1999b), the prospects for such radical institutional innovation at the global level are not bright, given the conservative proclivities of the G-7 (Akyüz and Cornford, 1999).

To the extent that there is extensive scope for institutional reform, it is at the domestic level. What became clear in the Asian and Mexican crises was the considerable lack of disclosure and transparency in both the public and private sectors, and the inadequacy of regulation and supervision in the financial sector. Such domestic reforms, moreover, have international impacts by reducing the risk and uncertainty faced by foreign investors contemplating lending or equity investment. In other words, more transparency, better regulation and workable bankruptcy procedures provide foreign creditors and investors with greater comfort as to the security of their investment and legal recourse in case things do not work out. These are precisely the areas in which most reforms are currently taking place and in which the World Bank is playing a leading role (Caprio and Honahan, 1999). However, these domestic reforms should not be confused with reforms of the *international* architecture. At best, they may be considered repairs to the plumbing.

Some important caveats are also in order. The history of the advanced industrial countries suggests that the institutional infrastructure required to oversee the efficient and equitable working of the domestic financial sector takes a long time to develop; and, as mentioned, it still does not guarantee that financial crisis will not erupt. There may be a problem with putting undue emphasis on domestic reforms in emerging markets if it leads to a widespread presumption that those destinations are thereby relatively safe for foreign investment. Thus, herding could still arise (leading to excess lending, asset bubbles and self-fulfilling panics), even as the problem of asymmetric information is resolved.

Moreover, regulation and standard-setting in the financial sector are evolving arts rather than immutable science. Just at the point that developing countries and emerging markets are being asked to adopt 'universal' standards of risk management, the industrial countries are moving to more flexible regulatory approaches based on assessing the sophisticated risk-management systems employed by banks and non-bank financial institutions themselves (Ahluwalia, 1999; Institute of International Finance, 2000). Finally, there is a rationale for not rushing the process simply in order to expedite financial liberalisation and openness to capital flows, since there is now a great deal of evidence to indicate that hasty financial liberalisation typically precedes banking and currency crises (Fanelli, 1998; Kaminsky and Reinhart, 1999).

What does constitute truly *international* reform? By definition, it is any reform to relationships between participants, public or private, in the international market, or to international institutions governing those relationships. Putting aside the creation of new institutions, the principal examples are: (1) the exchange rate regime; (2) rules governing capital flows; (3) the role of the private sector in crisis prevention and resolution; and (4) the policies and operations of the international financial institutions, particularly the IMF.

A UN Task Force reviewing the financial crisis in early 1999 provided a comprehensive articulation of the required scope of international reform (United Nations, 1999). It included firstly improving the consistency of the macro-economic policies of the major industrial countries, in order to reduce the possibility that they will collectively exert an inflationary or deflationary bias on the global economy. Secondly, it called for the provision of adequate international liquidity in times of crisis. The report suggested augmenting the IMF's resources via increasing its access to official funds, borrowing from the financial markets, and – a novel suggestion – by extraordinary and anti-cyclical emissions of Special Drawing Rights to countries experiencing crisis; such SDRs would be destroyed as they are repaid. Moreover, the Task Force argued for low-conditionality assistance from the IMF. In particular, IMF conditionality ' . . . should not include issues related to economic and social development strategies and institutions, which, by their very nature, should be decided by legitimate national authorities, based on broad social consensus'.

The Task Force also endorsed international codes of conduct, improved information and enhanced financial supervision and regulation, urging that they be applied to developing and industrial countries equally. It particularly emphasised preserving the autonomy of developing and transition countries with regard to capital account issues, and urged that controls on capital flows should not be regarded only as temporary instruments, as they now are by the IMF. It also argued for an internationally sanctioned 'standstill' provision to be incorporated into international lending, and for adequate sharing of adjustment costs with private investors.[1] Finally, it proposed strengthening regional and subregional organisations so that they could play a greater role in preventing and managing crises.

The reform agenda

Against this backdrop, we may now turn to the reforms under active consideration. The most comprehensive recent summary is contained in a report by the Acting Managing Director of the IMF, Stanley Fischer, to the International Monetary and Financial Committee (IMF, 2000b). The report puts considerable emphasis on 'key measures to ensure a more resilient international financial system', by which is meant enhancing transparency and accountability, assessing and enhancing members' standards[2] and codes (through ROSCs and comprehensive reports on standards and codes prepared in collaboration with the World Bank) and better identifying financial sector vulnerabilities.

These are precisely the set of reforms at the domestic level referred to above, designed to strengthen the ability of countries to withstand a greater degree of international financial turmoil. What of reforms to the international architecture? Firstly, the report also discussed the need to streamline the IMF's own facilities and increase its transparency. Both these proposals were major recommendations of the Goldstein and Meltzer reports.

Secondly, with respect to capital account liberalisation, the report says that 'progress has been made and discussions continue', but admits to 'differences of view on the merits of capital controls' and the 'need to carefully manage and sequence liberalisation in order to minimise risks'.

Thirdly, with regard to exchange rate regimes, the report recognises the difficult choice faced by most countries between, on the one hand, maintaining truly flexible rates and, on the other, 'hard' pegs (via a currency

---

[1] Canada has been a proponent of 'emergency standstill clauses' in debt contracts, which would give debtors the right to suspend payments for a specified period of time in the event of a financial emergency (Martin, 2000).

[2] For example, the Special Data Dissemination Standard developed by the IMF after the 1994–95 crisis.

board or common currency). Referring to the three major currencies (the dollar, yen and euro), among which flexible rates are likely to continue, it also points to 'large misalignments and volatility' in their exchange rates as being a cause for concern, particularly for small, open commodity-exporting countries. However, the report does not discuss any initiatives on the part of the international community, implying that the dollar-yen-euro relationship can only be sorted out between the USA, Japan and the EU.

Finally, with regard to involving the private sector, the report asserts that there has been some progress in working toward 'an operational framework for securing private sector involvement' in forestalling and resolving financial crises. It goes on to discuss the appropriate balance between IMF financing, adjustment policy and the role played by private sector creditors, emphasising the need to honour contracts as far as possible and to seek co-operative solutions to members' emerging debt difficulties. However, it hints that 'more concerted forms of private sector could be required if the financing requirement is large and the member has poor prospects of regaining market access in the near future or if the member has an unsustainable medium term debt burden' (IMF, 2000b: 15–16).

The contentiousness of the subject of private-sector involvement is evident from the report's tortured allusions to divided opinions on the IMF's Executive Board, as the following excerpt illustrates: 'Determining whether a debt burden is unsustainable is a judgmental exercise, and it could take time for the member and its creditors to reach agreement on the extent of the problem and its solution. In such cases, the IMF would be prepared to lend to a member in arrears to its private creditors . . . provided the member was negotiating with its creditors in good faith.' The report adds: 'Where private sector involvement is required, its precise form will have to be decided on a case by case basis'. It concludes: 'Only limited progress has been made in lifting institutional constraints to debt restructuring. Executive Directors encouraged the establishment of creditor committees if needed and on an *ad hoc* basis, and see merit in incorporating collective action clauses into international sovereign bond contracts . . . Directors considered that temporary and *voluntary* standstill arrangements could be desirable in some circumstances to minimise the risk of disruptive litigation, and some considered there should be further consideration of issues related to Article VIII, Section 2(b)' (IMF, 21000b:17; emphasis added).[1]

The only conclusion that can be drawn from this agenda is that the pre-

---

[1] This section of the IMF's Articles of Agreement has been invoked by those favouring a cessation of debt-servicing, sanctioned by the IMF as part of an adjustment programme.

scribed actions are long on domestic measures to reduce developing countries' vulnerability to financial crisis, while they are relatively short on measures that can be said genuinely to address the international architecture. There may be considerable merit in strengthening financial governance at the national level. But if the strengthening measures are premised on greater openness to foreign capital flows (albeit on a 'gradual and cautious' timetable), without stronger measures to exercise controls on capital markets (either at the national or international levels), they can also be viewed as half-measures. Such an impression is reinforced by a review of the initial work of the FSF.

The Financial Stability Forum

At its meeting in Petersberg, Bonn in February 1999, the G-7 Finance Ministers and Central Bank Governors endorsed the recommendation in the Tietmeyer report to convene a forum ' . . . to ensure that national and international authorities and relevant international supervisory bodies and expert groupings can more effectively foster and co-ordinate their respective responsibilities to promote international financial stability, improve the functioning of markets and reduce systemic risk' (Group of Seven, 1999a: para.15).

The first thing to note about the FSF is its composition. The G-7 communiqué added that: 'While the Forum will initially be the initiative of the G-7 countries, we envisage that over time additional national authorities would be included in the process. The issues to be addressed affect all countries, including both industrial and emerging market economies, and the G-7 regards this initiative as a step toward broader participation'. However, 'broader participation' clearly implied the inclusion only of the few countries most actively involved in global financial markets. For example, the countries or territories represented at the third meeting of the FSF in Singapore (March 2000) included, in addition to the G-7, Australia, Hong Kong Special Autonomous Region, Netherlands and Singapore. (It is worth noting that each of the G-7 countries was allowed three representatives, compared to only one from each non-G-7 country.)

In addition to national participants responsible for overseeing domestic financial stability, the Forum comprises representatives of the IMF, World Bank, BIS and OECD; representatives of the Basle Committee on Banking Supervision, the International Organisation of Securities Commissions (IOSC), the International Association of Insurance Supervisors (IAIS); and representatives of the two BIS-based committees, the Committee on the Payment and Settlement System, and the Committee on the Global Financial System. Fourteen of the 39 participants were officials from IFIs, International Regulatory and Supervisory Groupings and committees of central bank experts. The person appointed to chair the FSF was Andrew Crockett, General Manager of the BIS.

At its first meeting, the FSF commissioned three working groups: the first to address concerns related to highly-leveraged institutions (or HLIs, primarily hedge funds); the second on capital flows; and the third on off-shore financial centres. The working groups published their reports in March 2000 (Financial Stability Forum, 2000).

It is clear that the scope of the three FSF working groups was to examine some of the thorniest international aspects of the recent financial turmoil. Hedge funds, for example, were widely suspected of complicity in the speculative frenzy around the Asian crisis, including its spread to Hong Kong. And with the near-insolvency in 1998 of Long-Term Capital Management, the New York-based giant hedge fund, many of its US creditor banks narrowly escaped heavy losses. Had a concerted rescue not been organised by the Federal Reserve Bank of New York, the implications for the USA and world economies might have been very serious.

But in its report, the FSF working group on HLIs put most of its emphasis on enhancing the 'risk-management practices' and greater disclosure of counterparties and creditors to the HLIs, and of the HLIs themselves. (The latter is somewhat ironic, since most hedge funds are designed to be high-risk, high-return, closely-held and fairly non-transparent vehicles for very wealthy individual investors.) The group considered, but did not recommend 'at this stage', direct regulation of currently unregulated HLIs, although it kept the door open to this possibility if subsequent reviews pointed in that direction.[1]

The recommendations of the working group on capital flows followed suit; most of the emphasis was put on *managing the risks* to countries faced by greater capital flows. The group's assumptions were revealing: 'Industrial and emerging market economies alike share a common interest in building a strong and safe system for global flows of capital . . . A healthy capacity to mobilise external capital is critical to financing a growing and successful world.' From this follows the report's assertion: 'Realising the full benefits of capital flows will require adopting policies that control the risks associated with them'.

The report accordingly focused on urging emerging markets to develop

---

[1] An earlier report on hedge funds commissioned by the US President had also reached similar recommendations. *Hedge Funds, Leverage, and the Lessons of Long-Term Capital Management*. Report of the President's Working Group. Washington, April 1999.

sound practice guidelines for sovereign debt and liquidity management, and for management of official foreign currency reserves. In contrast, the report was rather critical about managing or controlling capital flows themselves. To begin with, it focused only on controlling inflows, emphasising the limitations of 'Chilean'-type inflow restrictions, even though these have been widely endorsed as a means of reducing the volatility of capital surges (see Edwards, 1999 for a critique of the Chilean system). And the Working Group did not discuss controls on capital outflows in depth. Such controls, its report stated, should be thought of more as an element of crisis management and, as such, were beyond the scope of the group.

Finally, the Working Group on Offshore Financial Centres (OFCs) concluded that, perhaps contrary to their reputation, these centres are not a major causal factor in systemic financial problems. It did, however, raise both prudential concerns and market integrity concerns (the latter referring to the facilitation of illicit activity by some OFCs). Its report was consistent with those of the other two groups in recommending the strengthening of transparency and disclosure and the adoption of international standards of behaviour by public authorities and private actors. It also encouraged onshore jurisdictions to engage in more effective consolidated supervision in banking and insurance where their activities involved dealings in OFCs.

In sum, while the scope of the FSF, and the work programme it has adopted, enables it to address some of the most difficult international dimensions of recent financial instability, the approach it has chosen clearly demonstrates a preference for risk management over 'behaviour management'. The rationale appears to be to reduce the vulnerability of countries subject to increasing volatility in the capital markets, rather than controlling the behaviour of those who are generating the problems. Given the highly selective composition of the FSF, with representation restricted to the world's leading financial centres and the world's financial regulators, this outcome may not be surprising. Thus, it could be argued that the FSF is biased in favour of liberalised and against regulated markets, reflecting the interests of its financial constituencies.

The G-20

In contrast to the highly select FSF, the G-20 comprises countries from throughout the world. The composition of the group has been carefully crafted: there are ten developing or emerging market countries, nine industrial countries comprising the G-7, Australia and the EU, plus one transition country, Russia.

As mentioned, the decision to establish the G-20 was taken by G-7 Finance Ministers in September 1999, when they committed themselves to ensure broader participation in discussions on international financial affairs among countries whose size or strategic importance gives them a particularly crucial role in the global economy.

It seems probable that the more inclusive G-20 was created, in part, to complement the more select FSF, and thereby deflect criticism that participation in the latter needs to be broadened to include some developing countries (Ahluwalia, 1999). In creating the G-20, the G-7 was clearly attempting to enhance the legitimacy of the decision-making process on international financial matters, a process which the G-7 has dominated over the past century (Porter, 2000).

But will it succeed? While it is reminiscent of the C-20 formed almost three decades ago to discuss fundamental international monetary reform, a stronger antecedent is the more recent G-22, with its focus on remedying financial fragility in countries at the periphery of the global system, rather than reforming the system as a whole or, for that matter, weaknesses in countries at the centre. Indeed, the initial focus of the G-20 is narrower than that of the FSF, which took on an examination of hedge funds, capital flows and offshore financial centres (although it resisted recommending any radical policy changes in these areas).

The relatively narrow orientation of the G-20 was evident even during its first meeting in Berlin in December 1999. The following summary indicates the kind of discussion that took place:

> Ministers and Governors at this inaugural meeting discussed the role and objectives of the G-20, and ways to address the main vulnerabilities currently facing their respective economies and the global financial system. They recognised that sound national economic and financial policies are central to building an international financial system that is less prone to crises. They noted the importance of strengthening national balance sheets to help cushion against unexpected shocks. They encouraged steps to strengthen sovereign debt management, and greater attention to the impact of various government policies on the borrowing decisions of private firms. They recognised that unsustainable exchange rate regimes are a critical source of vulnerability, and that a consistent exchange rate and monetary policy is essential. They discussed a range of possible domestic policy responses to the challenges of globalisation, and exchanged views on the role of the international community in helping to reduce vulnerability to crises.[1]

---

[1]G-20 Finance Ministers and Central Bank Governors Meeting, 15–16 December 1999. Available at http://www.fin.gc.ca/g20/news/001-e.html.

The four priority areas chosen for its work agenda were the following: (1) A comprehensive stock-taking of progress made by all member nations in reducing vulnerabilities to crises; (2) an evaluation by countries of their current compliance with international standards and codes in the areas of transparency and financial sector policy; (3) the completion of Reports on Observance of Standards and Codes (Transparency Reports) and Financial System Stability Assessments by the IMF with the co-operation of the World Bank; and (4) an examination of differing exchange-rate regimes and their role in cushioning the impact of international financial crises.[1] The similarity between this agenda and that of the G-22 working groups on enhancing accountability and transparency, strengthening financial systems and managing financial crises is quite striking.

Nor is the continuity with the work of the US-convened G-22 altogether coincidental. In a speech to the London Business School immediately prior to the first meeting of the G-20 which he was to attend, US Treasury Secretary Lawrence Summers stated: ' . . . helping countries to develop the capacity to realise the benefits of a global flow of capital and to manage its risks . . . is the goal at the heart of the global initiative that has come to be called the reform of the international financial architecture, which will take another step forward this week in Berlin as finance ministers and central bank governors from key industrial and emerging market economies gather for the first regular meeting of the G-20'. He went on: 'Refining our understanding of what makes countries vulnerable to modern-style crises and helping countries to guard against those risks will be a central focus for the G-20 as it carries forward its work'. He concluded: 'We believe that the IMF should work with member countries, including through the G-20, to develop and publish a set of explicit quantitative indicators that provide more meaningful guides to the adequacy of a country's reserves than simply their size relative to imports'.[2]

In other words, addressing domestic vulnerability to financial crises precipitated by capital flows appears to be the prevailing focus of the G-20. Even with respect to the one truly 'international architecture' issue, namely exchange-rate regimes, the discussion appears to be constrained to examining the choices available to developing countries along the spectrum from complete flexibility to 'hard pegs' through currency boards or currency unions.

---

[1]Press release, 'New G-20 Searches for Solutions'. Berlin, 17 December 1999.

[2]'The Right Kind of IMF for a Stable Global Financial System'. Treasury Secretary Lawrence H. Summers' remarks to the London School of Business, 14 December 1999.

Moreover, on this subject, the advice increasingly being given to emerging markets and developing countries is that 'corner solutions' (complete flexibility or 'hard pegs') are more viable than intermediate solutions involving managed flexibility. In practice, however, this advice amounts to a preference for 'hard pegs', since few countries are likely to be willing to countenance the volatility associated with complete flexibility. Furthermore, the question of the exchange-rate relationships among the three major currencies (the dollar, yen and euro) – relationships that have a profound effect on the rest of the world because of their trade, investment and debt with the three blocs – is not a subject for discussion.

It is hard to resist the conclusion that, so far, the G-20 is acting as a sounding-board for reforms endorsed by the G-7 and carried out with its blessing in the BWIs and the FSF. In this sense, the G-20 may embody the 'G7-isation' of international decision-making (Kirton, 1999) rather than a genuine broadening of participation. However, unlike the G-22, an ad hoc body with a short life span, the G-20 is as yet in its infancy, and the possibility exists of its non-G7 members taking initiatives and broadening its agenda.

Indeed, Canadian Finance Minister Paul Martin, the G-20's first Chairman, declared to the press after his appointment, 'There is virtually no major aspect of the global economy or international financial system that will be outside of the group's purview', an assertion he repeated when he appeared before a committee of the Canadian House of Commons (Martin, 2000). The scope for broadening the G-20's agenda will depend, in part, on which country is nominated to chair the group (in particular, whether a non-G7 country will ever be allowed to chair it). It will also depend on the willingness of the members of the G-7 to countenance a forum in which views are aired that are at variance with those of its principal members, notably the USA.

It is worth noting the striking contrast between the current 'architectural agenda' and that set out in 1999 by the UN Task Force. The current agenda is heavily weighted with financial concerns and interests and puts little emphasis on safeguarding the autonomy and welfare of the poorest countries and people. For example, the UN group emphasised that the exigencies of financial crises, serious as they are for the entire global community, should not crowd out funding for and international attention to, the problems of the poorest countries, and to the smaller countries as well. It asserted that 'strong protection for the poor during crises, through the design of effective safety nets, is still more a matter of rhetoric than of practice'. Moreover, it warned against diverting scarce, long-term development financing from such institutions as the World Bank and the regional development banks in order to provide liquidity to countries experiencing financial crisis (United Nations, 1999).

Conclusion: The Unfinished Global Reform Agenda and Regional Alternatives

For the past 40 years, global financial governance has been shaped by a 'flock of Gs' – the G-10, the G-5 and, finally, the G-7, which has ruled supreme during the last two decades. However, the core members of these groupings have always been the USA, Japan and Germany – the 'G-3'. In the 1990s the EU has taken the place of Germany in this triad.

With the calls for a 'new Bretton Woods' precipitated by the Asian, Russian and Brazilian crises, there were signs that the G-7 was finally prepared to engage more expansively in dialogue with the rest of the world; those aspirations have come to fruition in the Financial Stability Forum and the G-20. But as the above review of the work of these bodies to date indicates, there is little so far to suggest that the G-7 and the USA are not still firmly in charge of the agenda. Moreover, that agenda has been dramatically scaled back from discussion of genuinely international reform questions, which seemed possible at the height of the last crisis, to addressing financial fragility and vulnerability to crisis at the domestic level. While this approach is no doubt necessary to help countries cope with financial crisis, it hardly seems sufficient to help either prevent future crises or manage them.

Nevertheless, it is possible that these new deliberative bodies, particularly the G-20, perhaps with the leadership of some of its developing country members, might set off in a different direction. Hopefully, they might even address some of the larger challenges with regard to reforming the international financial architecture.

What are those challenges? Many were articulated by the UN Task Force summoned in 1998 to consider policy options to deal with international financial volatility (United Nations, 1999). They include:

◆   More universal surveillance of macro-economic and exchange-rate policies, including those of the G-3. The next crisis may be generated by current account imbalances and asset bubbles in this group, and the potential for a global crisis arising from sudden shifts in exchange rates and asset prices is large. So it is in the interest of the world community to try to engineer a 'soft landing';

◆   Transforming the IMF into a genuine lender of last resort, able to issue its own liquidity;

◆ More concerted approaches to debt restructuring, including the use of concerted payment standstills mandated by the IMF;

◆ A more stable exchange-rate regime – in particular, exploring options other than pure floating and 'hard pegs', for example, regional arrangements (see below);

◆ A more flexible approach to capital account liberalisation, including the development of policies regarding capital controls, not as instruments inexorably to be abolished, but as permanent safeguards that can be invoked, when necessary, by countries vulnerable to capital surges;

◆ Greater regulation of bank and non-bank flows (including portfolio equity and hedge funds);

◆ Greater country 'ownership' of adjustment policies adopted in crisis conditions;

◆ A thorough review and reform of IMF conditionality, particularly of the pervasive and intrusive sort evident in the Asian crisis.

This is a long list of extremely complex issues. The world has been struggling with all of them, off and on, for the past 40 years, as this paper's brief historical review has suggested. And it will not be easy to resolve any of them, certainly not quickly. However, if the G-20 is able to transform itself into a deliberative body that can help generate consensus on some of these issues, and if the G-7 is able to surrender the decision-making prerogatives it has enjoyed for the past two decades, there may be hope that over time the global financial architecture will be reformed in directions appropriate for the majority of the world's population.

Finally, if such global solutions are simply too intractable politically, it may be possible to register more modest progress on some of these issues by pursuing more regionally differentiated, or even less universal, solutions, rather than seeking global ones. Early on in the post-war period, the industrial countries, through the G-10, devised a mechanism, the GAB, that was designed as a first line of defence against currency crises in their own countries. Why cannot groups of developing countries do likewise? It is plausible that if regional groupings of developing countries come together to form their own 'self-help' groups, they may also serve to contain financial contagion in times of crisis by supporting all countries in the region. In so doing, they would also help prevent disruptions to regional trade and investment brought about by the crisis and by competitive devaluations. Finally, they could also engage in mutual surveillance, which would be far less likely to carry the imprimatur of

Washington-based institutions (Mistry, 1999).

Indeed, in the early stages of the Asian financial crisis, the Asian countries, led by Japan, discussed the possibility of pooling $100 billion of their resources in an 'Asian Monetary Fund' in order to stem the growing crisis and the possibility of contagion. Unfortunately, the plan was still-born due to the opposition of the USA; the Americans felt that the universality of the IMF should prevail. In principle, such an initiative would be no different from the GAB and NAB, but much better funded. Arguably, if such a facility had come into being, much of the ensuing turmoil and misery in Asia and perhaps the rest of the world would have been avoided (Wade, 1998).

The possibility of Asian monetary co-operation did not, however, die; indeed, it resurfaced in May 2000 during the annual meetings of the Asian Development Bank in Thailand. According to reports, a proposal backed by Japan, Korea and China to establish a network of bilateral currency swap arrangements and pooled reserves to defend regional members against currency attacks was endorsed by a broad group of Finance Ministers. Details are sparse, but it appears that Ministers agreed in principle to a regional initiative and to develop it further in due course. It is also worth noting that the idea was roundly criticised by several private bankers, including William Rhodes of Citigroup, who felt that the greater need in Asia was to follow through on the financial sector reforms required by the IFIs as part of the adjustment programmes agreed during the crisis.[1]

While Asian countries contemplate closer financial co-operation to fend off future crises, analogous solutions in other regions may be more complicated. In Africa there is no regional power like Japan capable of providing the bulk of the resources, although in this case the need for a short-term crisis facility may be less acute. In the western hemisphere, however, the country in the region most able to provide the resources necessary for crisis prevention or intervention (the USA) is the *least* likely to sanction such a scheme *ex ante*. It is more probable that the USA would intervene on a case-by-case basis when it sees its own interests threatened, as it did in Mexico in 1994–95.

In view of the political complexion of the region, a more controversial (and, to some, a more disturbing) approach to regional monetary co-operation in the western hemisphere may be achieved through 'dollarisation'. Advocates of this approach argue that fixed exchange rates (via

---

[1] Thomas Crampton, 'East Asia Unites to Fight Speculators', *International Herald Tribune*. Paris, 8 May 2000.

'soft pegs') were shown to be vulnerable to attack in the Asian crisis, and that truly flexible rates are an open invitation to volatility. That leaves only currency union (as with the euro) or currency boards (adopted by Argentina), both variants of 'hard pegs' (Hausmann, 1999). One obvious option, also being promoted by some prominent figures in the USA (Mack, 1999 and 2000), is unilateral dollarisation – an option chosen by Panama almost a century ago.

Advocates of unilateral dollarisation are growing in number. In February 2000, Ecuador, in the midst of an acute financial crisis, adopted the dollar. Debates on unilateral dollarisation are intensifying in many countries throughout Latin America, including Argentina, Mexico and smaller countries in Central and South America.

There has also been a debate in Canada, where proponents of dollarisation believe that ever-closer economic integration with the USA makes a common currency not only desirable, but inevitable (Courchene and Harris, 1999). However, these proponents advocate negotiating a common currency with the USA, along the lines of the euro, rather than espousing unilateral dollarisation. Critics of such a proposal argue, with some reason, that the analogy with Europe is far-fetched. Instead they contend there is very little likelihood that the USA would be interested in forming a currency union with its hemispheric neighbours and, further, that significant costs attach to unilateral dollarisation (McCallum, 2000; Sachs and Larrain, 1999).

The debate on dollarisation is likely to persist for some time. Even if no other countries formally dollarise, informal dollarisation, involving the growing use of the dollar for transactions and savings deposits and investment in countries throughout the region, is causing problems for macro-economic management (Helleiner, 1997). Meanwhile, other options for the region need to be explored, including the possibility of sub-regional monetary unions (for example, among the members of Mercosur or the Central American Common Market).

In the end, Hausmann (1999) might be right in asserting that a world with 105 currencies is an anomaly, one that has only met with limited success in the post-war period. A world with five currencies may make more sense and may even be more financially stable (Mistry, 1999). The problem, of course, is which currencies and how to get there from here. Finally, will such a system be any more subject to multilateral surveillance for the benefit of the entire global community than the present one, a virtual oligopoly of the G-3?

These questions require urgent research and policy attention in the coming months. But they also suggest the need for an alternative process of policy development, one that brings together researchers and practitioners from both North and South. The objective must be to seek viable policy alternatives for achieving and maintaining global financial stability – alternatives that attract the support of policy-makers in both the industrial and developing countries.

References

Ahluwalia, Montek S. (1999). 'The IMF and the World Bank in the New Financial Architecture', in *International Monetary and Financial Issues for the 1990s: Research Papers for the Group of 24*. Vol. XI. New York: United Nations.

Akyüz, Yilmaz and Andrew Cornford (1999). 'Capital Flows to the Developing Countries and the Reform of the International Financial System'. UNCTAD Discussion Papers, No.143 (November). Geneva: United Nations.

Bayne, Nicholas and Robert D. Putnam (1995). 'Introduction: The G-7 Summit Comes of Age', in *The Halifax G-7 Summit: Issues on the Table*. Halifax: Centre for Foreign Policy Studies, Dalhousie University.

Caprio, Gerard and Patrick Honohan (1999). 'Restoring Banking Stability: Beyond Supervised Capital Requirements', *Journal of Economic Perspectives* 13:4 (Fall), pp.43–64.

Collier, Paul and Jan Willem Gunning (1999). 'The IMF's Role in Structural Adjustment', *Economic Journal* 109, F634–F651.

Courchene, T.J. and R.G. Harris (1999). 'From Fixing to Monetary Union: Options for North American Currency Integration', *C.D. Howe Commentary* 127 (June).

Council on Foreign Relations (1999). *Safeguarding Prosperity in a Global Financial System: The Future International Financial Architecture*. Report of an Independent Task Force ('Goldstein Report'). Washington, DC: Institute for International Economics.

Culpeper, Roy (1999). 'Long-Term Financing for Development in the Presence of Market Instability'. Remarks to the Annual General Meeting of the Central American Bank for Economic Integration. 28 October. Processed.

Edwards, Sebastian (1999). 'How Effective are Capital Controls?', *Journal of Economic Perspectives* 13:4 (Fall), pp.65–84.

Fanelli, José Maria (1998). 'Financial Liberalization and Capital Account Regime: Notes on the Experience of Developing Countries', in *International Monetary and Financial Issues for the 1990s: Research Papers for the Group of 24*. Vol. IX. New York: United Nations.

Financial Stability Forum (2000). Reports of the Working Groups on Highly

Leveraged Institutions, Capital Flows, and Offshore Financial Centres. (April). Available at http://www.fsforum.org/Reports/

Fischer, Stanley (1999a). 'Reforming the International Financial System', *Economic Journal* 109, F557–F576.

Fischer, Stanley (1999b). 'On the Need for an International Lender of Last Resort', *Journal of Economic Perspectives* 13:4 (Fall), pp. 85–104.

Griffith-Jones, Stephany (1998). *Global Capital Flows: Should they be Regulated?* London and Basingstoke: Macmillan.

Griffith-Jones, Stephany with Jenny Kimmis (1999). 'The BIS and its Role in International Financial Governance', in *International Monetary and Financial Issues for the 1990s: Research Papers for the Group of 24*. Vol. XI. New York: United Nations.

Griffith-Jones, Stephany and José Antonio Ocampo with Jacques Cailloux (1999). 'The Poorest Countries and the Emerging International Financial Architecture'. Processed.

Group of Seven (1999a). 'Communiqué of G-7 Finance Ministers and Central Bank Governors'. Petersberg, Bonn, 20 February.

Hausmann, Ricardo (1999). 'Should there be Five Currencies or One Hundred and Five?', *Foreign Policy* 116 (Fall).

Helleiner, G.K. (1997). 'Capital Account Regimes and the Developing Countries', in *International Monetary and Financial Issues for the 1990s: Research Papers for the Group of 24*. Vol. VII. New York: United Nations.

Herman, Barry and Barbara Stallings (1999). 'International Finance and the Developing Countries: Liberalization, Crisis and the Reform Agenda', chapter 2 in Barry Herman, ed. *Global Financial Turmoil and Reform: A United Nations Perspective*. Tokyo, New York and Paris: United Nations University Press.

Institute of International Finance (2000). 'Leading bankers make major proposals to strengthen the international banking system'. Press release. The Hague, 12 April 2000.

International Financial Institutions Commission (2000). Report ('The Meltzer Report'). March. Washington, DC.

International Monetary Fund (2000a). *World Economic Outlook*. Washington, DC, April 2000.

International Monetary Fund (2000b). 'Report of the Acting Managing Director to the International Monetary and Financial Committee on Progress in Reforming the IMF and Strengthening the Architecture of the International Financial System'. 12 April.
Available at: http://www.imf.org.external/np/omd/2000/report.htm

James, Harold (1996). *International Monetary Co-operation since Bretton Woods*. Washington DC: International Monetary Fund; New York and Oxford: Oxford University Press.

Kafka, Alexandre (1994). 'Governance of the Fund', in *UNCTAD, The International Monetary and Financial System: Developing Country Perspectives. International Monetary and Financial Issues for the 1990s: Research Papers for the Group of 24.* Vol. IV. New York: United Nations.

Kaminsky, Graciela and Carmen M. Reinhart (1999). 'The Twin Crises: The Causes of Banking and Balance-of-Payments Problems', *American Economic Review* 89:3 (June), pp. 473–500.

Kindleberger, Charles (1996). *Manias, Panics and Crashes: A History of Financial Crises*, 3rd edn. New York: John Wiley and Sons.

Kirton, John (1999). 'What is the G20?'. Adapted from 'The G7, China and the International Financial System'. Paper presented at an International Think Tank Forum on 'China in the Twenty-First Century'. China Development Institute, 10–12 November.
Available at http://www.library.utoronto.ca/g7/g20/g20whatisit.html/

Krugman, Paul (1999a). 'A Dollar Crisis?' (1 August).
Available at http://web.mit.edu/krugman/www/

Krugman, Paul (1999b). 'Analytical Afterthoughts on the Asian Crisis'. (September). Available at http://web.mit.edu/krugman/www/MINICRIS.htm.

Mack, Senator Connie (1999). 'Encouraging Official Dollarization in Emerging Markets.' United States Senate, Joint Economic Committee Staff Report, Office of the Chairman. Available at http://www.senate.gov/~jec/dollarization.htm

Mack, Senator Connie (2000). 'Dollarization: A Guide to the International Monetary Stability Act'. United States Senate, Joint Economic Committee Staff Report, Office of the Chairman.
Available at http://www.senate.gov/~jec/dollaract.htm

Martin, Paul (2000). Speech to the House of Commons Standing Committee on Foreign Affairs and International Trade. Ottawa, 19 May 2000.

McCallum, John (2000). 'Engaging the Debate: Costs and Benefits of a North American common currency'. Royal Bank of Canada, *Current Analysis* (April). Available at http://www.royalbank.com/economics

Mishkin, Frederic S. (1999). 'Global Financial Instability: Framework, Events, Issues', *Journal of Economic Perspectives* 13:4 (Fall), pp. 3–20.

Mistry, Percy (1999). 'Coping with Financial Crises: Are Regional Arrangements the Missing Link?',in *International Monetary and Financial Issues for the 1990s: Research Papers for the Group of 24.* Vol.X. New York: United Nations.

Mohammed, Azizali F. (1999). 'Adequacy of International Liquidity in the Current Financial Environment', in *International Monetary and Financial Issues for the 1990s: Research Papers for the Group of 24.* Vol.XI. New York: United Nations.

Mohammed, Azizali F. (1996). 'Global Financial System Reform and the C-20 Process', in *International Monetary and Financial Issues for the 1990s: Research*

Papers for the Group of 24. Vol.VII. New York: United Nations.

Overseas Development Council (2000). *The Future Role of the IMF in Development.* ODC Task Force Report (April). Available at http://www.odc.org.

Porter, Tony (2000). 'The G-7, the Financial Stability Forum, the G-20, and the Politics of International Financial Regulation'. Paper prepared for the International Studies Association Annual Meeting, Los Angeles, California, 15 March. Available at http://www.library.utoronto.ca/g7/g20/g20porter/index.html/

Rogoff, Kenneth (1999). 'International Institutions for Reducing Global Financial Instability', *Journal of Economic Perspectives* 13:4 (Fall), pp. 21–42.

Sachs, Jeffrey and Felipe Larrain (1999). 'Why Dollarization is More Straitjacket than Salvation', *Foreign Policy* 116 (Fall).

Stiglitz, Joseph E. (1999). 'The World Bank at the Millennium', *Economic Journal* 109, F577–F597.

Tietmeyer, Hans (1999). 'International co-operation and co-ordination in the area of financial market supervision and surveillance', 11 February.

United Nations (1999). 'Towards a new international financial architecture'. Report of the Task Force of the Executive Committee on Economic and Social Affairs of the United Nations. New York, 21 January 1999.

United States Department of the Treasury (1998). *Reports on International Financial Architecture.* (October).
Available at http://www.treas.gov/press/releases/docs/g22-ltr.htm

Wade, Robert and Frank Veneroso (1998). 'The Resources Lie Within', *The Economist,* 7 November 1998.

Williamson, John (1977). *The Failure of World Monetary Reform 1971–74.* New York: New York University Press.

World Bank (2000). *Global Development Finance.* Washington, DC.

Appendix A. Conference Programme

THURSDAY 22 JUNE, 2000

10.00–10.30   **Future Challenges in Managing the World Economy**
Chair: Montek Singh Ahluwalia, Member, Planning
Commission, Government of India
Speakers: Dame Veronica Sutherland, Deputy
Secretary-General (Economic and Social Affairs),
Commonwealth Secretariat
Kemal Dervis, Vice-President, Poverty and Economic
Management, World Bank

10.45–12.00   **International Standards and Domestic Regulation**
Chair: Montek Singh Ahluwalia
Speakers: Jin Liqun, Vice Minister of Finance, China
Alastair Clark, Executive Director, Bank of England
John Hicklin, Senior Advisor, IMF
Shankar Acharya, Chief Economic Adviser, Ministry of
Finance, India

12.00–13.00   Discussion

14.30–15.30   **International Regulatory Challenges**
Chair: Dame Veronica Sutherland
Speakers: Lord Eatwell, President, Queen's College,
Cambridge
Philip Turner, Director, Emerging Markets, Bank for
International Settlements
Stephany Griffith-Jones, Deputy Director, Economic
Affairs, Commonwealth Secretariat
Avinash Persaud, Managing Director, Head of Global
Research, State Street Bank

15.45–17.00   **Private Sector Involvement in Crisis Resolution and
Impact on Capital Flows**
Chair: Gus O'Donnell, Head, Managing Director,
Macroeconomic Policy and International Finance,
UK Treasury
Speakers: Jack Boorman, Director, IMF
Robert Gray, Vice-President, HSBC
Pablo Guidotti, ex-Deputy Finance Minister, Argentina
Martin Wolf, Consultant Editor, *Financial Times*
Yung Chul Park, Professor, Department of Economics,
Korea University

FRIDAY 23 JUNE

9.00–10.45 **The Role of IFIs in a New Financial Architecture, Global and Regional Arrangements**
Chair: Caroline Atkinson, Senior Deputy Assistant Secretary, US Treasury
Speakers: Montek Singh Ahluwalia
Jose Antonio Ocampo, Executive Secretary, ECLAC, former Minister of Finance , Colombia
John Williamson, Senior Fellow, Institute for International Economics
Javed Burki, Chief Executive Officer, EMP Financial Advisors
Aziz Ali Mohammed, Adviser, G-24

11.00–12.30 Discussion

14.15–14.30 **Keynote address** by James Wolfensohn, President, World Bank
Chair: Don McKinnon, Commonwealth Secretary-General

14.30–15.15 **Capital Account Liberalisation and its Critique**
Chair: Javed Burki
Speaker: Y. Reddy, Deputy Governor, Reserve Bank of India

15.15–15.45 Discussion

16.00–16.45 **Conclusions panel:**
Chair: Amar Bhattacharya, Senior Adviser, Poverty Reduction and Economic Management Network, World Bank
Roy Culpeper, President, North-South Institute
Rumman Faruqi, Commonwealth Secretariat

16.45–17.30 Discussion

Appendix B. List of Participants

(alphabetical by family name)

Shankar ACHARYA, Chief Economic Adviser, Ministry of Finance, India

Montek Singh AHLUWALIA, Member, Planning Commission, India

Caroline ATKINSON, Senior Deputy Assistant Secretary, US Treasury

David BAKER, Associate of the Emerging Markets, Economic Unit, Financial Services Authority, London

H.E. Richard BERNAL, Ambassador of Jamaica to the USA

Amar BHATTACHARYA, Senior Adviser, Poverty Reduction and Economic Management Network, World Bank

Anil BISEN, Director, External Debt Management Unit, Ministry of Finance, Department of Economic Affairs, India

Jack BOORMAN, Director, Policy Development and Review Department, IMF

Howard BROWN, Director, International Finance and Economic Analysis, Ministry of Finance, Canada

Javed BURKI, Chief Executive Officer, EMP Financial Advisers, LLC

X. CIDERA, Institute of Development Studies, Brighton

Alastair CLARK, Executive Director, Bank of England, London

Melissa CRANFIELD, Counsellor, Economics, High Commission of Australia to the UK

Roy CULPEPER, President, North South Institute, Canada

Tarun DAS, Economic Adviser, Ministry of Finance, Department of Economic Affairs, India

Kemal DERVIS, Vice President, Poverty Reduction and Economic Management Network, World Bank

Rahul DHUMALE, Assisstant to Professor Singh

Mark DOBLER, Assistant Economist, Department for International Development, London

Cliff DOMMERS, HSBC, London

Lord EATWELL, President, Queen's College, Cambridge, UK

E.V.K. FITZGERALD, Director, Finance and Trade Policy Research Centre, University of Oxford, UK

Richard GOTTSCHALK, Institute of Development Studies, Brighton

Robert GRAY, Vice-President, HSBC, London

Barry HERMAN, Chief, International Economic Relations Branch (DPAD), United Nations

John HICKLIN, Senior Adviser, IMF

Xiao Ping JIAO, Assistant to the Vice Minister of Finance, China

Ana Maria JUL, Executive Director, IMF

Deanne JULIUS, Member, Monetary Policy Committee, Bank of England, London

Louis KASEKENDE, Deputy Governor, Bank of Uganda

Jenny KIMMIS, OXFAM, Oxford, UK

William KINGSMILL, Economic Adviser, Department for International Development, London

Guillermo LE FORT, Director, International Division, Central Bank of Chile

Donna LEONG, Economic Adviser, HM Treasury, London

Jin LIQUN, Vice Minister of Finance, Ministry of Finance, China

O.K. MATAMBO, Managing Director, Botswana Development Corporation

Colin MILES, Head of Economic, Data and Risk Analysis Department, Financial Services Authority, London

Aziz Ali MOHAMMED, Adviser, G-24, G-24 Liaison Office, USA

M.R. NAIR, Officer-in-Charge, Department of Economics Analysis and Policy, Reserve Bank of India

Gus O'DONNELL, Managing Director (Macroeconomic Policy and International Finance) and Head of Government Economic Services, HM Treasury

Jose Antonio OCAMPO, Executive Secretary, ECLAC, former Minister of Finance, Colombia

Yung Chul PARK, Department of Economics, Korea University

David PERETZ, Senior Adviser, Poverty Reduction and Economic Management, World Bank

Avinash PERSAUD, Managing Director, Head of Global Research, State Street Bank, London

Axel PEUKER, Economic Adviser, Poverty Reduction and Economic Management, World Bank

A. PRASAD, Executive Assistant to Y. Reddy, Reserve Bank of India

Y. REDDY, Deputy Governor, Reserve Bank of India

Benu SCHNEIDER, Fellow, ODI, London

Ajit SINGH, Queen's College, Cambridge

S.A. SPRATT, Institute of Development Studies, Brighton

Philip TURNER, Director, Emerging Markets, Bank for International Settlements, Switzerland

Rachel TURNER, Deputy Head, International Financial Institution Department, Department for International Development, London

Dwight VENNER, Governor, Eastern Caribbean Central Bank, St Kitts and Nevis

John WILLIAMSON, Institute for International Economics, USA

Martin WOLF, Consultant Editor, *Financial Times*, London

James WOLFENSOHN, President, World Bank

Shao Lin YANG, Deputy Director , International Department, Ministry of Finance, China